How to make a
WILDFLOWER
MEADOW

*To my parents, David and Susan, who instilled in me
a passion for nature and the countryside and then gave
me free rein with their farm and business to pursue it.
They also allowed me to destroy large areas of their
pristine lawns by turning them into wildflower meadows!
Thank you for giving me this opportunity.*

*And to my wife Claire and our boys Will and Olly. With much
love and thank you for your help, support and patience.*

New paperback edition published in 2022 by
Filbert Press Ltd
filbertpress.com

Designed by Kevin Knight

Printed in China

ISBN: 978-1-7399039-1-6

A catalogue record for this book
is available from the British Library.

How to make a
WILDFLOWER
MEADOW

James Hewetson-Brown

filbert press

Contents

Foreword

If you're anything like me you will by now have a collection of wildflower seed to rival the Millennium Seed Bank. Handed out at flower shows, stuck to magazine covers, given away with a jar of honey, wildflowers are on our minds as we hear about the lack of food for honeybees and other pollinators.

But achieving a wildflower meadow that fulfils your expectations in terms of colour and longevity, returns reliably year after year and brims with wildlife is no slam dunk. A big shout out therefore for James Hewetson-Brown and this book, which brings a refreshingly pragmatic note to the wildflower meadow debate. His state-of-the-art techniques including his much celebrated wildflower turf (star of Chelsea Flower Show and the London Olympics) are practical, reliable and show you how to make a meadow you can enjoy the year you plant it rather than in 5 years time.

Some of this is about being clear about what a meadow is and what is reasonable to expect from it through the seasons and year after year – you can read more about that in the following pages. But more importantly this book explains how a lot of the unpredictability of meadow-making can be overcome by choosing the right application method – whether that's roll-out turf, seed or 'naturalizing' – and implementing an appropriate maintenance regime, particularly when it comes to cutting.

But who has space for a wildflower meadow? I'm always surprised to see statistics that show how, when put together, even small meadow areas in back gardens make a significant contribution to replacing the wildflowers we've lost due to intensive farming after the Second World War. These small plots in gardens, parks, suburbs, cities and main roads provide 'wildlife corridors' that allow species to travel and become healthier through access to a wider gene pool. These habitats are not just for insects either but provide nesting places for small mammals and prey for animals further up the food chain.

Meadows are also good for people. The philosophy of this book is that meadows should be enjoyable to make and bring pleasure year

after year. At least one of the meadow makers featured in the book describes his meadow as 'a way of life'. Meadows are for humans as well as wildlife and walking through waist-high flowers and grasses brings a sense of well-being and close contact with nature that is hard to beat.

Alys specified wildflower turf for the Peninsula Garden in south-east London to create this biodiverse environment that is good for pollinators and people.

Alys Fowler

PART ONE
Introduction

Why plant a meadow?

A wildflower meadow can conjure up romantic visions of rolling landscapes where colourful, dainty flowers reveal themselves as you wander through a sea of grass on a lazy sunny day. The dictionary definition is a little more prosaic: "a meadow in which a large range of perennial native flowers and grasses coexist from one year to the next". This species-rich habitat is historically found on soils with poor fertility. Managed by a cutting regime, a wildflower meadow is a long-term, sustainable, biodiverse environment. In the UK, about 2,500 native species can be found, although they are thinly spread these days. Whatever the definition, there's no denying that for people it's a habitat that can offer a sense of well-being and a tranquil escape from the stressful aspects of modern living.

A wildflower meadow is a spectacle in flower and provides a valuable food source for pollinators.

Wildflower meadows tell a fascinating story of how landscapes have evolved over time. A product of gentle intervention through early agriculture, they have lost out to modern intensive farming, population growth and industrial development. At times, wildflowers have been taken for granted and regarded as unwelcome arable weeds, but the significant changes in the way that we live and the demands on our land mass have resulted in a dramatic loss in biodiversity. Fortunately, we are seeing a revival of wildflower meadows, with decisive action to halt the decline in biodiverse environments. There is a realization that meadows do not just provide a romantic link to the haymaking days of the past, they are also intrinsically connected to the future health and well-being of both humans and wildlife.

Creating a meadow, either small and intimate or a large-scale panorama, is a significant achievement. The pleasure of getting back in touch with nature and playing a part in the survival of a heritage landscape has encouraged many to give it a go. Whether you are a time-poor suburban gardener looking for a low-maintenance solution, an ecologist keen to provide essential wildlife habitat or a landscaper who needs a long-term solution for a client, wildflowers are likely to be a viable solution. They will bring benefits no matter the size of your project, from a few patio boxes to acres of parkland.

However, the current enthusiasm for wildflowers has to be tempered by an understanding of them and the practicalities of their establishment and maintenance. For some reason, 'wildflowers' is a term that seems to imply that human intervention is unnecessary. This may be the case in specific, natural habitats but these are rare and only found where the influence of humans is negligible. On the whole, and certainly in our temperate climate, there is work to be done to achieve a species-rich and colourful habitat that suits wildlife and humans. Some images of brightly coloured annuals labelled as wildflowers on seed packets do not accurately depict what a real-life wildflower meadow will look like. These products can set the wrong expectations of meadow-makers throughout the land and do more harm than good when hopes are not met.

Gardeners' perceptions of wildflower meadows range from the realistic naturalized grassland that might have a few flowers in the summer to the unrealistic wall-to-wall colour for 12 months of the year. There is a tendency to think that as much colour as possible is the ultimate success, but should we regard species diversity as the

Right: A strip of meadow beside a coastal footpath.

Below: Wild flowers associate well with ponds to create habitats for wildlife.

Above: The use of non-natives can add vibrant colour particularly when using an annual seed mix but will not have the longevity of the natives below.

Left: A mix of annual and perennial native wildflowers provides impact and longevity.

definitive indicator instead? There is no right or wrong answer to that, but an understanding of what is achievable will lead to expectations and results being more evenly matched. It is the repeated failure of wildflower projects and the disillusionment that many experience when their well-meant project turns into another weedy mud patch that I want to address with this book. If the meadow-maker gives up it is a wasted opportunity for all concerned, not only for the owner, designer and contractor but also for the bees and butterflies.

This book does not set out to provide you with the science behind the plants, or tell you which species happily coexist, flower for the longest time or are best suited to certain conditions – I shall leave that to the botanists and plant ecologists, who have spent years studying such things. This is about getting those people who want to enjoy wildflowers to cross the threshold from an aspiration to a successful meadow. It will look at planning, establishment and maintenance to provide a long-lasting wildflower landscape. It is my intention to make meadows easier to understand and achieve by sharing my experience of different situations and application techniques.

This is the first book to look at both the traditional and modern methods of meadow creation and I hope it is both inspiring and useful for home gardeners, ecologists, architects, garden designers, landscape contractors, planners and public space guardians. All of

Top: Even a small strip of wildflowers like this one between the lawn and the path will benefit wildlife.

Above: Wildflowers flourish up high on a green roof.

Left: A wildflower area attracts a ringlet to the garden.

those sectors have different reasons for creating a meadow but the required result is common to all: a meadow that establishes quickly and provides a long-term beneficial landscape for humans and nature.

While the practical elements of the book concentrate on the establishment of a perennial meadow, I want to be able to help you decide what type of meadow is right for you. Considerations include the choice of native and non-native species as well as the impact of annual wildflowers. You will need to know how to plan your site and prepare the ground according to the method of installation you choose. An illustrated step-by-step guide will take you through the different methods of installation and subsequent maintenance required and there are suggestions on how to enhance your meadow through additions such as bulbs. Of course things can go wrong along the way and I hope the practical guidance on problems with meadows will help you identify and rectify any problems that may occur.

At the heart of the book are real-life case studies, a catalogue of meadow-making experiences. The 30 different projects range from novice gardeners planting a new section of a front garden to schools creating outdoor classrooms and award-winning garden designers providing inspiration with wildflower meadows now famous around the world. There are wildflower roofs pushing architecture into a more sustainable future and landscapers creating biodiverse spaces where nature had all but disappeared. I think there are lessons to be learned from every story. Each project details the motivations for, and planning of, the meadow, the methods of establishment, any problems encountered and a thoughtful review of the success of the meadow.

My aim is that both the practical information and the case studies will equip you with what you need to plan your meadow and maintain it. Ultimately, a wildflower meadow requires work – a 'hope for the best' approach won't be successful! I hope that the work will be a labour of love as you create your own version of a landscape that allows us to tread lightly on the land and, rather than compete with nature, engage with it to leave a lasting and beneficial legacy.

Top: Wild flowers flourish in towns and cities.

Above: A low-maintenance meadow works in a shared garden.

The history of wildflower meadows

Wildflower meadows of one sort or another have been around for a long, long time. As landscapes emerged from the hold of ice age glaciers, wildflowers would have been one of the early colonizers. Conditions would have been harsh and soils would often have been low in nutrients, giving perfect conditions for wildflowers to flourish. Annuals were the first to establish with perennial plants quickly taking over. As the soil developed with the breakdown of vegetation, a richer topsoil developed. This began to sustain more plant life and shrubs took over, hogging more nutrients and light and restricting the space for wildflowers. The look of the landscape slowly started to change as the soil developed sufficient depth to support trees and much of the landscape eventually turned to woodland. While catastrophic events such as volcanos, earthquakes or forest fires would have created bare soil to start this process again, large-scale wildflower meadows and prairies shrank to specific areas sustained by distinct and individual circumstances.

The link between agriculture and wildflower meadows

As human civilizations developed so did the demand for shelter and food. Woodland was cleared for firewood, construction and agriculture and this offered opportunities for wildflowers to return. Eventually, farmers became inadvertently responsible for large areas of wildflower meadow by leaving the grass to grow in the spring in order to harvest hay in the summer. Autumn and spring grazing would open up grass swards offering the opportunity for perennial wildflowers to establish, while cultivating land for cereals and vegetables provided ideal conditions for annual wildflowers. Where bare soil was exposed, poppies and cornflowers would have been a regular sight in the spring and summer before harvest. These agricultural practices prevented shrubs and trees from getting established and as fertilizers and pesticides had yet to be developed, a species-rich, wildflower-friendly environment was assured.

While agriculture remained at little more than subsistence levels, these husbandry systems kept the nutrient levels in the soil to a minimum and allowed wildflower habitats to thrive. In turn, these diverse and species rich environments encouraged a wide range and abundance of wildlife.

However, with population growth and an increasing demand for food, more efficient production techniques were continually developed. In time, farmers turned to using herbicides and fertilizers and this was particularly apparent during and after World War II with the realisation that food security was vital. Agricultural research and development became critical objectives across the sector and led to widespread use of pesticides. Higher grain yields and better quality were the target for the arable grower, while the livestock farmer wanted more grass for the animals that provided meat and milk. These pesticides were designed to optimize conditions for the food-producing plants and left no space for the less productive wildflowers.

Historical agricultural practices, particularly hay-making, provided an ideal environment for wildflowers to establish, as a by-product of the cutting regime.

The casualties spread quickly, resulting in the current much used statistic that the UK has lost 97 per cent of its wildflower meadows since World War II.

The modern landscape

In 2013 a report looking at The State of Nature was compiled by 25 conservation groups. The report revealed that 60 per cent of British native species are in decline and one in ten are heading for extinction. Agriculture was blamed but in addition, housing, road-building, industry and the need for maintained public space have all added pressure to the demand for land and were signalled out as contributors to the decline. This loss of biodiversity has until recently gone virtually unrecognized. We cannot escape the need for land for growth, development and food, but we must accept that we cannot continually change landscapes for our use without replacing the biodiversity that is lost. Experts have always understood the importance of biodiversity, but the recent widespread recognition of the speed of its decline has reinforced the realisation that something positive must be done. More recently, media coverage has generated a public appreciation of the importance of bees and butterflies and other pollinators and this more general awareness and understanding offers some optimism.

Farmers are obliged to provide biodiverse habitats through European and Government incentives. Farmers consider themselves as custodians of the landscape and would like to ensure a healthy environment from one generation to the next, but it is their business to supply food and their produce is desperately needed. Consequently, planners, landscape architects and developers should be encouraged to regard our urban landscapes as an opportunity to provide these environmentally beneficial habitats. Over the latter half of the twentieth century, the 'mown look' was everywhere. Large areas of lawn grass were thought to be accessible, while verges had to be maintained to look neat and tidy. This orderly look led to vast areas of land being preserved as green monocultures, devoid of species variety and valueless for wildlife. It is time to accept less manicured urban areas and appreciate the cyclical beauty of wildflowers and the importance of flora for the benefit of fauna.

In 2014, the National Pollinator Strategy published by DEFRA (Department of the Environment, Fisheries & Rural Affairs) brought to light the plight of the 1500 pollinating species that we rely upon

The demand for neat and tidy urban monocultures is making way . . .

for much of our food production and biodiversity. This is one of many initiatives now having a profound effect on the interest in wildflower environments.

Biodiversity

The term 'biodiversity' describes the variety of plant and animal life in a particular habitat, a high level of which is considered to be fundamentally important. Each plant species and creature plays a vital role in the circle of life, interdependent for a range of necessities from food and shelter to oxygen and soil enrichment. Maintaining and enhancing biodiversity is central to the challenge of sustainable development. Edward O. Wilson, known as the father of biodiversity, said, 'It is reckless to suppose that biodiversity can be diminished indefinitely without threatening humanity itself.' (*The Diversity of Life*, 1992).

What is a sustainable landscape?

. . . for more areas of species-rich habitat.

For a landscape to qualify as truly sustainable, its maintenance must require the minimum of non-solar inputs of energy, materials and labour. This is difficult to achieve in modern society and compromises have to be made. Some inputs are required by wildflower meadows but they are sustainable landscapes and their development is vital. Monocultures, such as lawns or paved areas, are not environmentally sustainable and do not address biodiversity loss. An established meadow is resistant to weed invasion and greatly reduces the need for maintenance, fertilizers, watering or replanting, which means that it meets the above definition in all but its autumn cut.

There is no doubt that we should be encouraging a range of landscapes and no one type of naturally occurring flora should be held in higher regard than another. Most developed countries are working towards a plan of maintaining existing woodlands, meadows, marshes and moors. But in areas where development has led to extreme biodiversity loss, wildflowers are certainly the quickest way of returning a species-rich environment to the land. No other type of low-maintenance landscape would give equivalent biodiversity in terms of the number of species of flora and fauna and offer such opportunity for long-term habitat improvement.

Biodiversity in urban landscapes

Those who are responsible for landscape planning and design can make significant changes to urban biodiversity. Through the late twentieth century, the fashion for more exotic plants became evident in towns and cities. Planting schemes that were supported by a ready supply of labour and chemicals were the result and native plants that had already suffered from habitat fragmentation, vanished in urban areas.

What had been large areas of biodiverse habitat became divided and subdivided into smaller fragments which are either completely isolated or destroyed altogether through ongoing development. Where larger areas of underdeveloped land within urban areas did exist, those responsible for them were working with tight financial constraints and timelines. The way in which these areas were designed and maintained has been fundamental in retaining, or losing, biodiversity. Mown parkland can be created quickly and cheaply, but not only does it provide little in the way of habitat and food for fauna, the monoculture of grass soon generates large on-going maintenance bills due to the continual mowing and care it requires. The future of urban biodiversity is still very much in the hands of planners and architects and they are essential to help develop new approaches consistent with sustainability and biodiversity.

There are many opportunities to develop and enhance biodiversity in urban and semi-urban areas. A wildflower meadow can provide instant biodiversity due to the species-rich nature of its make-up. In today's culture, where instant results are demanded, using wildflowers in domestic gardens, green roofs, highways, parks, cemeteries and so forth is a way of packing a great deal of 'biodiversity punch' into relatively small areas within a very short timescale.

Wildlife and wildflowers

One of the many benefits from the establishment of a wildflower meadow is the associated wildlife that you will encourage to the

area. The extensive plant diversity attracts butterflies, bees, insects, invertebrates, birds and mammals with a ready supply of both food and habitat, often offering a complete ecosystem in its own right.

Land around this railway station provides an opportunity to introduce wildflowers to an urban neighbourhood.

The successful establishment of this delicate chain of fauna is directly related to the abundant food supply that exists within a wildflower meadow. Plant material and nectar are a food source for many invertebrates including bees, butterflies, moths and other insects. These insects, along with seeds from plants, form the diet of many small birds such as finches, yellowhammers and linnets and they are particularly important for their young in the summer.

For example, at our farm in Hampshire in England, there is a flourishing population of nocturnal moths, which provide a healthy supply of food for both little owls and bats. Many birds of prey including barn owls, red kites, kestrels and buzzards hunt across the open fields and meadows in search of voles and shrews, which in turn visit our wildflower meadows in search of beetles and small insects. It is clear to see the food chain at work, from the vegetation to the top predators, in any biodiverse environment, whether rural or urban.

Certain species have evolved to rely upon a specific habitat type or food source and once their habitat changes they will struggle for survival. Some can certainly adapt but fragmentation does cause population decline. Those that are unable to adapt are forced to migrate or die off. Populations of the same species become cut off from one another as their natural habitat is decreased or blocked off with a physical barrier. A road, housing development, industrial structure or even a fence can prevent a normal pattern of movement. Species that would normally follow a fairly mobile existence retreat into patches of habitat, causing additional pressures in the form of increased competition and a reduced gene pool. Smaller fragments of habitat support smaller populations which are therefore even more vulnerable to extinction.

Habitat creation

The vegetation that exists within a wildflower patch forms a protective shield for many forms of wildlife, offering shelter from the elements as well as from predators. The wildflower environment is a fairly consistent habitat from year to year and with the minimal maintenance required, it ensures a long-term fixed area with minimal disturbance for a wide range of fauna.

The key to making successful wildflower areas that conserve wildlife lies in the provision of a solution that ticks the boxes for the landowner or those responsible for land management. This applies whether you are a domestic garden owner or local authority managing a city park. A wildflower space needs to work well for the landowner to ensure that they keep it forever. The form it takes will depend on the requirements of the landowner but in general it needs to look appealing and be easy to look after! If this is achieved and the landowner is happy, the area will provide the essential plant mix and variation for insects and animals forever and everyone wins.

Wildlife corridors

The joining-up of beneficial habitat is essential for broadening the genetic pool of many species and even the smallest wildflower spaces throughout a town or city can provide migration channels so that

Hares frequently make use of meadows for nesting.

animals and insects are not stuck in one spot. Conversion of a space within a back garden is a wonderful idea to encourage wildlife into your garden, but councils, highways agencies and railway companies can play a huge role in creating green corridors along transport routes that allow animals and insects to move freely.

A species-rich environment provides habitat for a huge range of wildlife. The kestrels featured here are at the top of the food chain and benefit from this meadow and its biodiversity.

Reintegrating species

Modern techniques of establishing a wildflower meadow, such as using wildflower turf, can be particularly useful for mitigating the impact of new building developments on flora and fauna. Timing is essential for providing a suitable home, as existing communities of wildlife such as slow worms or newts will need a very quick reinstatement of habitat. Wildflower turf can be installed and a new environment created and established in a number of weeks. It is also possible to re-create a habitat using this method by including the type of seed mix appropriate for a particular animal population. This speed of establishment combined with

Left: Deer will graze and use a meadow as cover.

Below left (centre): Late-flowering plants such as this teasel provide important food sources for the bee population.

Below: A small tortoiseshell butterfly using the common knapweed as a rich source of nectar.

Below left (bottom): Wildflowers are magnets for many pollinating insects including this hover fly.

Above left: Newts found colonizing a new urban meadow.

Above: Barn owls scour meadows for prey.

Left: Peregrine falcon looking for prey within a wildflower meadow.

An attractive roadside verge and an urban green corridor which supports wildlife.

the possibility of site-specific species can work to reinstate a habitat or establish a short-term home for the translocation of wildlife while development work is done. While it is possible to get site-specific seed mixes to suit certain wildlife, the time taken for this seed to establish will be too slow for the dependent fauna.

Understanding the relationship between flora and fauna

During the course of developing my wildflower turf, I was determined to try to enhance biodiversity when compared with the lack of diversity found in the monoculture of a lawn. Establishing the relationship between species diversity of the fauna and of the flora was an important step.

A reasonably good-quality lawn will have a very limited number of species and varieties of grass and can certainly be described as a monoculture. It is a one-dimensional environment with little height to provide habitat for anything but the smallest of insects and very limited as a source of food. In the wildflower turf I eventually developed, there are 34 different plant species each with different growth habits, from height to flowering dates. A truly three dimensional habitat offers many more opportunities for shelter and food for a wider range of fauna. The results of our studies showed direct correlation between the numbers of species of flora and those of fauna.

Over the years we have been working with wildflowers, the direct relationship between the diversity of species and the amount of wildlife has been commented upon by many of our clients. It is easy to walk into a wildflower meadow through any of the warmer months and see phenomenal insect life at a glance. We also have many stories of the wider range of wildlife from slow worms to field voles, mammals and birds of prey. The links from the bottom to the top of the food chain can be evident in even the smallest of meadow areas.

Biodiversity in the modern landscape

Today, many gardeners and most landscape professionals want a way to establish wildflower meadows quickly and reliably. The establishment methods recommended by many wildflower enthusiasts are founded on historic techniques that have done little to improve the take-up of wildflower meadows. Results have been limited and we hear a lot about how hard it is to create a wildflower area and that 'we tried it, it didn't work and we gave up'. For the decline of wildflowers to be reversed and the enthusiasm for them to be maintained, a modern method that is quickly implemented is needed.

It is unlikely that we shall ever get back to the wildflower areas that existed post-World War I, but what we can do is ensure that the areas that we do reinstate are even more beneficial than those in place a hundred years ago. Many of the larger naturalized areas would have been lacking in species diversity but we now have the desire and opportunity, as well as the tools, to give much better results in smaller areas. This will result in better-quality wildflower meadows and a much bigger benefit to biodiversity. While the constraints of modern society with its demands for food housing and recreation will continue to take precedent over environmental ideals, there is no excuse to ignore the opportunities that do exist to ensure a balance is maintained. Wildflower meadows may remain rare and highly prized but we have an opportunity to give them a helping hand.

PART TWO
Practicalities

Choosing the right method

Let's take a look at the different establishment methods that can be used to create a wildflower area. Which you decide to choose will depend upon your site, budget, time and enthusiasm for the work involved, as well as how long you are prepared to wait to see results.

Natural regeneration of grassland

This method, often referred to as naturalizing, can be used on an area of existing grassland or lawn. In its simplest form, it means that whatever grasses, wildflowers or weeds are already in the site or that naturally migrate to it will be allowed to grow with just the cutting regime as the main management intervention. With a change of management techniques, seeds that have remained dormant in the soil for years may decide the time is right to make an appearance.

However, by leaving things entirely to nature, you of course relinquish control over what may grow and it is likely that while biodiversity will be increased over the years, the overall appearance of wildflowers maybe less satisfying and the number of species limited, certainly in the short to medium term. While there is a minimal amount of work and effort involved with this method, the timescale is certainly years and not months and the overall look, without intervention, is more likely to resemble an unkempt grass meadow rather than a colourful wildflower meadow. The higher grass content of this meadow type still provides a reasonable wildlife habitat but you might need to enhance the meadow with plugs to give it more visual impact and improve biodiversity. With knowledge, enthusiasm and a great deal of time, naturalizing can be a great approach. It is a low-cost method that is satisfactory as long as you have realistic expectations on the amount of time it will take and the quantity of flowers you can expect to see.

Plugging

Plugging is the insertion of individual, pre-grown wildflower plants into your selected area and is a technique that can be used on its own or as a top-up for other methods. Plugs of different sizes can be used,

Naturalizing is a long process; don't expect an abundance of flowers too quickly.

but subsequent establishment is best when the plants are already of a good size (2 litre or ½ gallon pots) as they have more energy to persevere in a competitive environment, while smaller plug plants may be overtaken by existing plants in the same way seeds can be.

The major downside of this method is that while you can see quicker results, it requires a huge number of plants and a lot of work to install them. Few people adopt it because of the cost, particularly when establishing larger meadow areas. However, plugs are an excellent way to enhance and improve an existing wildflower meadow, as they help to develop species diversity and increase the colour of the area; they are a great tool for augmenting and enriching rather than creating from scratch. Note that if wildflower plugs have been cultivated in a manipulated climate such as a greenhouse or polytunnel they need to have a period to harden off before planting out in the autumn or early spring.

Seeding

Sowing seed of perennial wildflowers is a long-term commitment – one of my wildflower seed suppliers has likened it to creating an apple orchard, where you can only expect fruit five years after establishment. It is a step on from the naturalizing process in that you start with nothing and choose the species hoping they will germinate and establish. The visual result is likely to be quicker than natural regeneration, but the area will have other influences that are often out of your control and most of these can be detrimental to the success of seeding. Weather-related problems such as high winds, heavy rains and too much or too little heat will all have an effect on germination. Sowing time – autumn or spring – and day length will influence species variety and establishment rates. Birds and animals can damage or eat vulnerable seedlings, soil types will have an impact on what is successfully established and by creating a new seed bed you are certainly going to awaken existing weed seeds that are already present in the soil. Furthermore, the quality of the seed you buy, both purity and germination rates, will have a huge effect on the success of seedling establishment, as will soil compaction and seedling disease.

As you can see, the start of a seeding project can be fraught with problems but even with the many risks associated with seeding it is

Above left: Plugging can be rewarding for integrating rare species but is most successful when topping up an existing meadow.

Above: This meadow has been enhanced with cowslip plug plants.

If you intend to seed a perennial meadow, you must plan ahead and include a robust maintenance regime to ensure the wildflowers succeed over time. The key maintenance requirement of a seeded meadow is regular mowing and collection of arisings.

still a favoured method, largely due to the perceived lower costs. Once your seeds are established, expect a lot of ongoing work in order to get the best from the species you have introduced. Cutting, removing and weeding will keep you busy for the first 3–5 years. It is rare to hear of long-term success with perennial wildflower seeding that doesn't involve a lot of detailed planning, followed by hard work over a number of years. When everything is in the meadow-maker's favour, from a low weed seed content in the soil to low soil fertility, it can work. This may be by chance or through meticulous long-term planning.

It is possible to get better seeding results with annual wildflowers as they are quick to establish and more able to compete with the weeds. Non-native species in particular are competitive and have been bred and developed to deliver reliable results.

Hydroseeding

An alternative application method for seeding a wildflower meadow, hydroseeding in essence still requires the same amount of work and time to create a successful wildflower environment. The application of seed is quick using this technique and involves a coloured slurry or liquid mulch made up of water, fibres, some organic material and a tackifier or glue. Seed is added to this liquid and applied to the soil with a spray gun. The slurry is fired under high pressure through the gun and when it hits the soil, the tackifier sets to hold the mulch and seed in place.

This system was developed for seeding steep banks. It has the advantage of ensuring that seed dispersal rate is reasonably accurate and it is a quick way to cover large areas and often areas that are relatively inaccessible. It does require specialist machinery and has to be done by a contractor. It will not help with many of the issues mentioned above but will assist with stabilising the top soil and is useful for slopes.

Turfing

Using a pre-grown wildflower turf is a relatively recent introduction in the establishment of wildflower meadows. As a modern technique it has the benefit of a history of research and development and has been tried and tested to give optimum and reliable results. The first

high-tech stage in the development of a wildflower meadow, it introduces a mat of nursery-grown pre-established wildflower plants that have been specifically chosen and set in appropriate quantities to provide an even distribution of species. The turf is developed using a manufactured growing medium which is inert, and therefore entirely free of weed and grass seeds that might compete while the wildflowers establish. Unlike seeding, there is much more of a guarantee that the wildflowers in the turf will thrive when introduced to the receptor site because they are so well established.

The result is a complete meadow, much further along its evolutionary journey than one could hope to get after 10 years of naturalizing or 5 years of seeding. You can specify exactly the mix of seeds that you would like and if local provenance of seed is important it is possible for the meadow-maker to collect seed to create a site-specific wildflower turf. Not only are you more likely to have success with the plants that you do want, but you also have more control over the plants that you don't want. The turf is a densely networked root mat that supports the healthy, established and instantly competitive

Hydroseeding is a quick way of establishing meadows on a bank. The harmless green colouring is a cosmetic aid, designed to make it look as if there is plant coverage while the seeds germinate.

Wildflower turf is a mat of pre-established mature plants. Once in contact with the soil, these wildflowers are quick to send their roots deep into the soil. This is a reliable method of creating an instant meadow.

wildflowers above it. The massed density of roots in the turf mat act as a weed-suppressing carpet, smothering any seeds in the soil beneath that might be on the point of germinating.

While this is the most guaranteed method of creating a meadow, the up-front cost is higher than seeding. It is perfect for the meadow-maker wanting immediate, guaranteed and risk-free results.

Wildflower earth – a modern approach to seeding

The latest advancement in meadow-making, wildflower earth bridges the gap between seeding and turfing. This innovative idea for establishing a wildflower meadow is a pre-mixed seeded growing medium that combines many ingredients to give optimum germination conditions for wildflower seed. It is unique in meadow creation as it requires little ground preparation and for that reason is low in cost due to minimal labour requirements. It is suited to larger meadow projects and amenity landscapes where budgets are tight and relatively quick results are required.

The pre-seeded growing medium has special agents that lock in moisture and sufficient nutrients for fast germination and establishment. This gives the wildflower plants the opportunity to be rapidly competitive against the plants that you don't want. It is light and quick to apply, with no need to disturb the ground before installation. After a methodical application of glyphosate to kill the existing weeds and grass in an area, the wildflower earth is applied as a layer over the top of the dead area of vegetation and this forms an effective barrier to the weed seeds that are present in the soil. This method requires no soil rotovation and no tilth creation, which goes a long way towards preventing the start of weed seed germination in the parent soil and to keeping the costs down. This gives the wildflowers in the pre-seeded growing medium a chance to germinate before the grasses and weeds get a chance to re-establish themselves. If you prefer not to use glyphosate, the same results can be achieved by stripping off the top layer of turf using a turf cutter. This has a similar outcome – it removes the growing plants and weeds to leave bare soil that has not been cultivated, ready for immediate installation of the seeded growing medium.

This new development simplifies the establishment process

Successful meadows are all about quick and robust establishment. Modern techniques and products such as wildflower earth, are evolving to meet the demands of the new meadow makers.

while providing a level of certainty about the speed and success of germination. You also have more ability to choose your own seed mix and add in seeds of local provenance if required. Unlike the turf, it is season-specific and is preferably applied in the spring and autumn. Wildflower earth is appropriate for larger areas that are easily converted from grass to meadow.

Choosing a method

The enthusiasm for wildflower meadows has never been greater, but the process of establishing them is always underestimated. Whichever method you adopt the resultant landscape will be a wildflower meadow of sorts, but the variables will be the work and time involved, the costs, the range and diversity of species that are present and the look and visual impact of the meadow. Having realistic expectations is vital, as is a thorough plan before starting – and if you are creating the meadow on behalf of someone else, make sure they are aware of the likely outcomes. Great results can be achieved by using any one of the methods, but weigh up how quickly you want to see results, how much time you have to dedicate to the project and how much knowledge and effort it will take to prepare and install the meadow.

Planning a wildflower area

Before going ahead with any wildflower project, it is well worth considering the reasons you are choosing wildflowers, what can be achieved and in what timescale and then planning the area accordingly. This will help you decide on the type of meadow that would most suit your needs and expectations and the methods that you should adopt to create it. Here are some specific environments and ways to plan them, although many of the considerations are common to all locations.

Domestic gardens

Look at the patch you have in mind and how it relates to the rest of the garden and buildings on the site. Then, before making any decisions as to how you set about creating your meadow, consider the following questions.

What is currently growing on the plot of land?

This will give you an indication of fertility levels as well as the amount of work that will be required to clear the site in preparation for wildflowers. If it is currently a mass of weeds, you must consider how best to clear them for an effective weed-free start for the wildflowers. The weed seeds in the soil will be considerable if the area is already very overgrown and weedy. These weeds can be cleared over time by digging them out as they appear but it may take a while to do this thoroughly. If time is of the essence a glyphosate application will clear the plot effectively, though if the weed seed burden of the soil is high one application may not be enough. Creating a false seedbed and allowing the area to regrow before giving a second application of glyphosate is a very useful technique to improve weed control. But even with two or three applications, a very weedy area is hard to clean up in one season and in these circumstances seeding is probably not the best option.

Wildflowers will grow in most soils and situations, but be careful with heavily compacted areas that are prone to waterlogging. Wildflowers can withstand long periods of drought but if roots are in

standing water for a long period of time, it's likely some of the species will not survive.

Wildflower meadows are particularly well suited to inaccessible areas such as slopes, which are hard to work and mow.

How accessible is the area?

If the site includes slopes or banks this will affect the installation method as it can be difficult to create a suitable tilth. Heavy rain and recently seeded banks are not a good mix, particularly where soil isn't free-draining. If the bank is south-facing, the time to start the project is in the autumn to maximize establishment before the possibility of a dry spring limiting the wildflower growth. Accessibility may limit the management of the meadow. Think how it will be cut and cleared before deciding on a site.

Impactful colour schemes are often desired, particularly in domestic garden situations. Seed suppliers are working on mixes to try and achieve colour impact along with the plant longevity found with natives.

Will shady areas affect the growth of the plants?

Wildflowers don't necessarily require direct sunlight to thrive, but they do need a reasonable amount of light; heavily wooded areas giving continual shade through the summer will not suit them. If the area receives only very limited light through the day you may need to consider remedial work in the form of crown or canopy lifting and think of the mix of wildflowers that are best suited to these conditions. There are plenty of shade-tolerant wildflowers and it is possible to grow successful meadows in areas of shade beneath trees, provided certain conditions are met. Shade from walls or buildings is less of a problem as the area is likely to get ambient light through the year and will still benefit from the longer summer days. In a wood, a dense leaf canopy prevents this and has a detrimental affect. In addition leaf drop plays a major part in slowing or stopping wildflower growth as the leaf litter is just another form of unwanted competition.

What sort of visual impact do you want?

Is your heart set on an area that is vivid in colour or would you prefer a subtle and natural colour palette? This will help to determine your choice of annual or perennial wildflowers and native or non-native species.

Public green spaces

The reasons for establishing wildflowers in public spaces are likely to be similar to those for a domestic garden but there will be further considerations because more than one party will probably be involved. These parties will all have specific aspirations they want the meadow to meet:

• Ecologist – plant species suitability/diversity and how will they benefit wildlife?

• Landscape architect/designer – does it have the desired aesthetic appeal?

• Landscape contractor – will it be easy to install and will it give me guaranteed, stress-free results?

• The landowner or governing body – what will it cost, how long will it take, how is it maintained, and will the public like it?

Along with those already described for domestic gardens, other considerations include:

• How is the area currently used and how does this affect the installation and establishment method? A roundabout or verge is not really in use, whereas an urban play park will require cordoned-off areas to allow meadow establishment. So the level of public access is likely to have an impact on the establishment method as time will be of the essence to limit any disruption.

• Is the area being created with an aim to help wildlife? This not only has an impact on the choice of plant species used but also in encouraging the public to interact with the area once created. Would the use of interpretation boards be of benefit to both the site and the public? Paths to give access to the meadow should be planned in a way that limits disturbance to wildlife.

• Is your budget a one-off sum or an ongoing annual allowance? This will determine whether you choose annual or perennial species. There will need to be resources to maintain either choice. It is important to understand what is involved with establishment and upkeep for both.

• Who will be responsible for the maintenance programme? Before

A seeded annual meadow seen at the 2012 London Olympics delighted visitors. Annuals are a reliable source of colour but only for one year.

the project is started, a plan must be put in place for maintenance so that the wildflowers will continue to thrive past the first year. Low maintenance doesn't mean no maintenance and all successful wildflower meadows need hands-on management year after year.

• How big is the area and what sort of machinery can the site take for installation and maintenance? How safe is access, if the site is a roundabout or verge? Wildflowers have the advantage that access would be needed for only one cut per year.

Once all parties have been consulted, it is important to understand and manage expectations before going ahead with the project. Crucially, a wildflower area is an ever-changing scene through the year and will not produce flowers non-stop. An understanding of annual or perennial wildflowers will have a bearing on the colour, longevity and management of the meadow. Time spent considering the options and planning accordingly will be time very well spent.

Annuals or perennials

The choice between annuals and perennials is an important one, as they have very different lifecycles.

An annual wildflower, such as a poppy, cosmos or cornflower, is a one-hit wonder, a total show-off. It has to put all of its energy into being very attractive for pollination purposes, as its chance to produce seed is all that it has in order to ensure ongoing survival. The plant only gets one go at this as at the end of flowering its life is over, so its key characteristic is often bold colour and it may have a prolonged flowering season. The seed produced then lies dormant in the soil until suitable conditions occur. In order for this seed to grow the following year most annuals will require the topsoil to be worked to produce a tilth. The classic example of an annual wildflower is the field poppy, which became the emblem for Remembrance Day after World War I. The disturbance of the soil during battle gave perfect growing conditions for poppies and they were so prevalent over the trenches and bomb craters that they came to represent this and subsequent wars. However, without annual soil disturbance few poppies will grow. If you see a poppy on the verge or in the garden, the chances are that something, from a spinning tyre to the scratching of a rabbit, has created bare soil to give suitable conditions for it to grow.

Perennial wild flowers, such as common knapweed (*Centaura nigra*) and field scabious (*Knautia arvensis*), live for more than two years so they have to invest in energy to survive through the winter. This can be either as rootstock, or as a winter hardy plant. As a result, less of the plant's energy goes into the flower so the flowering season can be shorter and the colours more subtle. Perennials have a number of features to help them survive for more than two years. Vegetative reproduction means that the success of the seed is less vital and deep roots help the plant to survive in difficult conditions such as droughts or unusually cold winters. So perennial plants are hardy once established and are ideally suited to a long-term meadow. If you're ever unsure about whether a plant is an annual or a perennial, a quick test is to get hold of it and pull. An annual will come out of the ground with relatively little effort, while a perennial – unless very young – will stubbornly resist letting go of the soil!

An understanding of both annuals and perennials makes choosing one or the other easier. Having both isn't really an option other than in year one. Putting annuals in a perennial seed mix does give extra first year colour but can make expectation unrealistic for subsequent years. I often hear comments such as, 'We loved the meadow in the first year, but it has never been as colourful since.'

Making the choice

Annual plants will require a good seedbed to give perfect growing conditions. If everything goes well there should be a great display through the summer. The plants will die off over winter and it will then be time to start the process again. The same preparation and sowing will be required to get the same results the following year. While self-sown annual seed can be viable it does require the creation of a tilth to germinate. Most people decide that once they have gone to the trouble of preparing the soil they are reluctant to rely on last year's seed alone and they tend to boost the area with another sowing of annual seed.

Perennials will provide a green base for the whole of the year and for this reason are probably suited to larger areas. Their roots tend to be thicker and deeper rooting and so once they are established it is harder for weeds to get underway and they will continue to grow year on year without the need for much maintenance, other than an annual or biannual cut. The colours can be less vibrant than annuals but are beautiful in a subtle way and the permanent, undisturbed root zone and habitat is very beneficial to wildlife. In addition the lack of soil disturbance is a very good carbon sink – ploughing or rotovating the soil will contribute significantly to realeasing carbon into the atmosphere.

As you can see from the pictures there is quite a difference in look and feel from annual to perennial wildflowers and while many may be drawn to the colour of the annuals, there is certainly more involved in maintaining the display. Annuals are fantastic for high-impact public displays such as those used at the London 2012 Olympics but for long-term, low-maintenance and reliable meadows, the perennials would be a better option. Apart from the first year, annuals and perennials won't mix unless managed as described, so there is a clear choice to be made

at the outset of any wildflower project.

The meadows at the 2012 Olympics and other inner-city landscape projects have clearly captured the public's imagination and have significantly contributed to the growth of interest in wildflowers. But are annual mixes really wildflower meadows and are they likely to be maintained year on year in the way described? If not there is a danger of setting expectations too high, with a resultant loss of interest as the implications of maintaining an annual display become apparent.

Native perennials are beautiful with their subtle colour palette. They provide longevity and a perfect species-rich habitat for wildlife.

Natives or non-natives

There are opportunities for the best of both worlds with non-native perennial meadows that can offer the vibrant colours of annuals with the longer-term survival characteristics of perennial plants. This recent and exciting development combines the visual requirements of colour and flowering duration with the low maintenance and low costs associated with the native perennials. Plants for Bugs was a four-year field study conducted by the Royal Horticultural Society Science Department at Wisley and supported and inspired by the Wildlife Gardening Forum. The study looked at the relationship between insects and native, near-native and exotic plants. In short, results showed that insects didn't mind which plants provided them with food and habitat. However, I have yet to be convinced that some of the non-native plants that are currently on offer have quite the staying power of native wildflowers.

The debate about native vs non-native planting has developed as interest in wildflowers grows, particularly among those protecting and providing habitat for pollinators. In the last few years ecologists planting for biodiversity and wildlife have not considered anything other than native species. As a result specifications and regulations have driven a species choice that is of local provenance or at least British provenance. However, more recently and certainly in more urban areas, the demand for colour has led to the use of non-native varieties. So where should you stand on the native vs non-native debate, what should you be doing on your patch and how important is it to source your seed or plants from your locality?

Plants for Bugs was the first-ever field experiment designed to test whether the geographical origin ('nativeness') of garden plants affects the abundance and diversity of wildlife they support. The study measured how much fauna was found in the different planted areas and checked whether there was any difference when planting native, non-native northern hemisphere species or exotic species (southern hemisphere). It was aimed at helping domestic and professional gardeners, designers, ecologists and others working in the horticulture industry make the best choices for our fauna and is also relevant when deciding on the type of wildflowers to use in any urban or suburban landscape.

Interestingly, the results showed that variety is the key: a wide range of species will deliver greater variety of fauna irrespective of whether the plants are native, near-native (naturalized but not native to the UK) or exotic. The study concluded that emphasis should be given to plants native to the UK and the northern hemisphere, though exotic plants from the southern hemisphere can be used to extend the flowering season. Therefore there is no right mix of wildflowers – they are just a habitat to be encouraged and the more plant biodiversity you have, the more fauna you will get. The reality is that in most gardens, the areas designated for wildflower planting are not big enough to have an impact on the native flora and fauna. It is only in large country gardens and semi-natural areas around the countryside where the cultivated areas need to reflect the adjoining semi-wild areas; in such locations non-native planting will have an obvious effect, along with the potential to invade the native areas.

If you choose non-natives in your mix a delayed cutting time can be appropriate since they may flower later in the season and provide a more vivid flush of colour. Otherwise there will be little variation in terms of the overall management. We know that native wildflowers are incredibly hardy and will flourish throughout the year, having resilience to seasonal extremes and also pests and diseases that naturally occur within our gardens. Non-natives in a wildflower meadow context have yet to prove themselves on all of the above. In time, the resilient non-native species will become apparent and be used more often as a result.

My belief is that being too prescriptive about whether natives or non-natives are best may put people off planting any wildflowers at all, and this will be at the expense of wildlife. Surely it is better to have a perennial covering of wildflowers whatever their origin than none at all – with the caveat that existing native meadows that are species-diverse should remain just that!

Design and preparation

Whether you are designing a meadow yourself or hiring a professional garden or landscape designer, there are a few basic principles that help with the process. A wildflower area will add a new level and texture to the landscape and provide an ever-changing look at a height of about 1 m (3¼ ft) through the summer. It is important to visualize your design in three-dimensional form so you can think about the viewpoints from different aspects of the garden. Consider how much of a focal point you want the wildflower area to be and also what it might block from view when at its full height.

If you are designing the garden yourself, it is really useful to draw at least a simple sketch that gives some sort of proportion. This will help you to picture the size of the area appropriate for wildflowers; in the same way that you would not want only trees or lawn, a garden with only wildflowers will look uninteresting. Instead, make the area another feature, one that will affect the whole character of the plot. You might want it to be a quieter section that is set back and this could include a space where you can sit and immerse yourself in nature. Wildflower areas will suffer if subjected to a lot of wear so it's best not to position yours at the edge of a busy play area, as it is likely to be flattened by balls and little feet – and you may fall foul of lost balls when it comes to cutting time!

Desire lines

Desire lines, or desire paths – the easiest route to a destination – are an important consideration. Is the meadow on a route that is regularly used in the garden? If you place it between the garden shed or greenhouse and the back door, for example, make sure there is a path designed to give access. This applies to compost heaps, gates and play areas as well as any regular destination (in our case the hen house). If your wildflower area will border any of these, it is sensible to think about paths during the initial planning stages. Paths with straight lines or curved edges can both look good, depending upon the design of the rest of your garden and the size of the meadow. The wildflowers will

grow tall and hang over a path, so allow an adequate width of at least two runs of the mower to give yourself room.

Most importantly, remember that at some point through the year the wildflower area will need to be cut with a mower or strimmer and the clippings removed. Edging the area with gravel or similar loose surface coverings might not be appropriate when you think about the practicalities of mowing. Using bricks or pavers for a path can work well, but keep them level with the meadow to make mowing easy. The path could be traditional lawn turf or you could regularly mow a path within the wildflowers so it just becomes a ribbon of species-rich lawn.

Wildflowers can enhance the design of a garden, softening edges of new builds, creating borders and providing a new layer of interest among the cultivated species.

Right: A mown path allows you to navigate a meadow and provides an interesting design detail.

Below: Take time to sit and enjoy your meadow.

Seating areas

If the size of your wildflower area allows a path for access, the immersive experience is wonderful. Part of the appeal of a meadow is to sit within it and look at its ever-changing scene. There are always different plant species to spot from month to month, as well as the wildlife that will inhabit the area. Install a seating area and you will find yourself pleasantly whiling away the hours. Add a camera to the mix and it is easy to spend hours getting the perfect shot of a bumble bee with its dusting of pollen, or a hoverfly in sharp focus.

Adding trees to the design

Trees within a meadow look great and wildflowers are of particular benefit to fruit trees. The flowers will provide a good source of nectar to pollinating insects, encouraging them to stay in the area ready for the flowering of the trees; not surprisingly, the higher the insect count the better the pollination of the blossom on the fruit trees and the more fruit there is to eat.

With most trees, there comes a substantial amount of leaf litter and debris. It is essential that this is removed in autumn to prevent adding nutrients back into the soil in the form of rotting vegetation. This also ensures perennial wildflowers have access to light and air to keep them healthy. If you do not want to have to pick up leaves and fruit on a regular basis, either avoid planting the wildflowers in this area or leave an adequate margin around each tree – young trees will in any case need a margin of at least 1 metre (3¼ ft) radius in which to add mulch to help the health of the tree. Mulch is preferable to low grass around a tree as the latter will require cutting, which could prove difficult if it is surrounded by wildflower meadow. Grass will also be competing for the nutrients and moisture that the tree needs for growth.

Hedges and edges

If your wildflower area is going to be on the periphery of your garden, think about how it flows on to what's next to it – a pond, hedge, wood or field, perhaps. If access is required to cut back hedges or trees then practically speaking you will need a margin to avoid the wildflowers encroaching onto the hedge. Allowing for a margin of mown grass against a hedge makes for a sharper look and emphasizes the fact that the meadow is a deliberate part of the design of the garden.

Trees and shade-tolerant wildflowers are a winning combination.

Measuring

Once you have decided upon your design, you will need to know the area that the meadow will cover. Measuring the area accurately is important and it is worth doing this twice and probably a third time! This will ensure that you order and apply the correct quantities required to achieve the best results.

Some parts of the garden may be difficult to measure so allow a margin for error. Corners, irregular edges of flowerbeds and the borders around trees or other features are easier to measure if you break them down into compartments. Plotting the area on graph paper with a scale can improve accuracy. Once plotted, you can count the number of squares within an irregular shape on the graph paper to give the number of metres required.

Ground preparation

It is the ground preparation that is likely to take the most amount of time in the process of creating the meadow and neglecting to do this properly could have consequences for the success of the meadow. The more time you can dedicate to site preparation the more likely you are to give the wildflowers the best start. There is an old farming adage that goes 'One year's seed gives seven years of weeds.' If you are not thorough with the treatment of weeds in your proposed site at the beginning, you will inevitably be dealing with them throughout the lifetime of your meadow. However, if you are methodical in your approach to ground preparation you will have done 90 per cent of your work to create your meadow at this stage.

Creating a margin between meadow and fence is useful for maintenance purposes.

Consider how you will prepare your site. If your site is a mass of weeds, be sure that you have the time, machinery and know-how to clear it properly.

If the proposed area is a mass of brambles and weeds you must weigh up the work involved to clear it back to weed-free bare soil. If you are not prepared to be thorough from the outset you should properly lower your expectations of the resultant meadow.

Inhibiting weed growth

Preventing light and moisture from reaching an area by covering it with a layer of black plastic or other light-blocking material is a method that can be used on a small scale for those wanting to avoid employing machinery or chemicals. However, it's hard to imagine that anyone would want this sort of covering in a domestic garden for a long period of time as it is unsightly and can blow about unless well pinned down. As soon as the sheet is taken off, dormant seeds in the soil will get going again, so act quickly!

Systemic chemicals

A systemic chemical such as glyphosate, commonly bought as 'Round Up', is the cheapest and easiest method of ground clearance for all sorts of sites and is particularly useful where machinery is unable to access an area. It is quick and reliable and the least complicated of all ground preparation methods. Glyphosate is the active ingredient and this inhibits a specific enzyme in the plant to stop it from growing. It is active on allgreen leaf material, so use with care; once in contact with the soil it becomes inactive.

It is understandable that many would prefer not to use chemicals for weed control. While glyphosate has been in use for the last 40 years, it has its share of detractors and has recently come under attack over safety issues. While there are reports of it having negative effects on the food chain, there is still very little scientific evidence to say that there are ongoing health risks to wildlife and humans. I am of the opinion that if the site is a mass of weeds providing limited visual appeal and inadequate biodiversity, the benefits of introducing a wildflower meadow far outweigh the use of a tried-and-tested chemical. The end result is a truly beneficial habitat that should last for ever and require no further input of any chemical whatsoever. Leaving an area covered for more than a year to stop the growth of weeds is far more damaging to the indigenous wildlife population and unless you are extremely thorough with any of the other methods of weed control you may well be compromising your chances of success and find yourself with the choice of giving up the wildflower meadow or having to start again.

Use glyphosate on a dry day and apply it to a dry leaf. For it to work effectively, the area must remain dry for 24 hours after application. Results should be visible within 10 days; the treated area will start to die off and change colour to a yellow-brown. The area can then be rotovated to install seed or turf or left alone for the application of a pre-seeded growing medium.

Stripping with a turf cutter

If the area you are clearing in preparation for wildflowers is a lawn, using a turf cutter is a relatively straightforward method of ground clearance. Areas of lawn make a great starting point for a wildflower meadow as the weed seed burden in the soil will be relatively low. This is because regular mowing helps to check weed development and

If you are applying glyphosate, follow product guidelines, wear protective clothing and use appropriate equipment.

the competitive nature of a lawn will limit the amount of viable weed seed inherent in the soil. A turf cutter simply removes the top layer of soil and vegetation and leaves bare earth. It is a mechanical piece of kit that can be easily hired. The level can be set to skim off an even depth of turf and topsoil. You will be left with bare soil that can then be be dug over or raked to a tilth, depending on how compacted the underlying soil is.

This method would not work so well on an area that was highly colonized by weeds as the machine would struggle with any roots that are more robust than those of grass. And unlike the action of glyphosate, simply cutting the roots will not guarantee that the plant dies – rhizomatous and stoloniferous plants will send up new growth from remaining roots without any green leaf being present. But, it does leave a clean soil that can be ready to use without the need for much more work and I would definitely consider this option. Of course it does produce lawn turf that will need to be dealt with – either rehomed as a new lawn or composted to produce topsoil.

Stripping with a digger

This is a method for a large-scale project and particularly useful for landscapes that are uneven, very stony or have been neglected to allow the development of substantial weeds, shrubs or small trees which have taken hold. Clearance will be quick but the cleared soil will still require a reasonable tilth and a digger will struggle to do this in one pass.

Creating a tilth

Once you have achieved bare soil there are a number of ways to create a tilth, the required depth of which will depend on the state of the soil. If it is very compacted you will need a fork or rotovator to dig deep and break up the soil so that the roots of the wildflowers can easily penetrate the earth for moisture and nutrients. A mechanical rotovator is particularly useful for heavily compacted sites and will prepare your area much quicker than manual methods.

Where the bare soil is light and loose you may well be able to rake it over to create a tilth without having to work it with a fork or rotovator. When using turf to create your meadow, a fine, even tilth is less of a requirement as the coverall nature of the turf is quite forgiving and will camouflage any imperfections. Pull out the big clods of soil, stones and

Left: Stripping turf is relatively quick and allows you to easily demarcate the area for your meadow.

Below: Creating a tilth with a mechanical rotovator will ease the amount of work, but raking afterwards is advised to break up large clumps of soil.

For large sites it will be necessary to use appropriate ground preparation machinery.

roots as these can impede the establishment of the wildflowers. The soil should now be ideal for the next stage.

For a large site, using heavy machinery is the easiest way of preparing the soil. Agricultural contractors will be accustomed to manipulating soil to get the best results for seeding and using their expertise and equipment will make life easy!

Sourcing your seed

If you have decided to sow your own meadow, the quality of the seed will play a large part in its success. Currently in the UK, there are no official seed standards for wildflowers, so how clean the seed is (is it made up with inert material?), its purity of species (does it include weed seed?), and its germination (the viability of the seed) is rarely tested. This is unlike grasses, which are thoroughly tested for all the above. It can be hard to test for seed germination as some wildflower seed relies on specific conditions to break dormancy, such as an extended cold spell, but seed of unknown quality does not help with successful establishment. Harvesting seed of any type is not easy, even when the weather is on your side and spells of wet weather will make seed collection very difficult. Harvesting in a wet year affects seed quality due to damp seed losing viability in the field and during post harvest storage. These variables will result in seed that is not consistent in quality and with no testing of any sort, it is impossible to be sure how viable the seed is when bought. However, it is worth asking the question at the time of purchase and there are some suppliers who will offer germination tests. It might cost a little more but will give much greater confidence.

There is also the debate about the provenance of the seed. Should it be local, or from anywhere in the UK, or can it be grown abroad? This is a decision for you, but I recommend making sure that the seed is wild and avoiding any agricultural cultivars. An example of this is red clover. Agricultural varieties grown for forage are very aggressive and will grow much more rapidly and robustly than native wild red clover.

Grass content

Finally, the grass content of a wildflower seed mix is an important factor to think about before sourcing the seed. In simple terms, the greater the grass content of the seed mix, the cheaper it will be. However this obviously means there will be more grass growing in the meadow and you risk smothering many of the wildflowers. To maximize species diversity and for successful wildflower establishment, use very little grass seed – 25 per cent is plenty – and use non-aggressive grasses only. It is very easy to add grass at a later date, and much harder to remove it.

Your perennial meadow – what to expect and when

It is surprising how many people think that a wildflower meadow is full of vibrant colour, flowering for 12 months of the year. Knowing what you are letting yourself in for is key to the long-term survival of a wildflower meadow and the benefits it will bring to associated wildlife as well as to your own well-being. A meadow is an ever-changing scene, from season to season and year to year, and will vary according to the geographic location as well as climatic conditions. This pictorial guide is therefore an indication of the lifecycle and seasonal change of one meadow with a specific seed mix, in one year and with a one-cut regime.

If you are able to harvest locally grown seed you will know that it is more likely to grow well on your site.

What to expect from a perennial meadow

1 Early April: emerging from winter dormancy.

2 Mid to late April: rapid growth starts.

3 Early to mid-May: the first flowers emerge with a flush of colour.

4 Late May to mid June: a denser sward of flowers shows with vibrant colour.

5 Late June to early July: in full flower, although some early flowers are starting to set seed.

6 Mid to late July: early flowers senescing and some late flowers such as knapweed beginning to show.

7 August to September: grasses seeding with some late wildflowers showing, but still a beneficial habitat.

8 Mid September to October: cut back and leave to green up over the winter period, then start the cycle again.

Installation techniques

You will have discovered the pros and cons of the various ways to establish a wildflower meadow. This chapter explains how to be successful with your chosen method.

Creating a meadow from seed

Starting your meadow from seed can be a very rewarding task, but it does require a fair amount of knowledge and will certainly be a more time-consuming project – if you are hoping for a perennial meadow, expect to be working on your project intermittently for 3–5 years before you can enjoy the finished article. For all good meadow establishment, site preparation and getting quick and robust plant growth are essential. These two steps will have the biggest influence on success.

When establishing a meadow by seed, you will need to create an appropriate seedbed that has been rotovated to a fine and even tilth. In order to achieve this, the soil should be completely clear of existing vegetation, including roots. Some species of wildflower require surface sowing, but to protect the various types of species in the seed mix and give them the best chance of germinating, lightly raking the soil after sowing will help to ensure good seed-to-soil contact which will improve overall germination. The soil should then be lightly rolled to help lock in any moisture and firm the area against wind erosion.

Of course, the ideal preparation for the sown seed is also ideal for any weed seeds that are left in the soil and these will germinate quickly too. They are generally aggressive and are likely to out-compete the wildflowers. It is worth repeating: take every opportunity to clean the site before sowing and make sure that you sow at a time when the wildflowers can establish quickly, so avoid sowing too early or too late in the season.

Timing

Time is of the essence when seeding a meadow and it is often overlooked. Ground preparation will always take longer than imagined and so it is important to start planning your meadow early. You have two ideal windows of opportunity when seeding a meadow: early spring and late summer/early autumn. Sowing too early or too late will reduce the amount of daylight available to the germinating seed and will also have a bearing on the warmth and moisture levels of the soil.

Top tips for seeding

• Store the seed in a cool, dry, dark spot before use to keep germination rates at their best.

• Thorough weed control is important. If using chemical control methods, wait for 4–6 weeks after the treatment for any second flush of weeds. Then you can do a final clearance of any new weed seeds that have germinated before you sow the seed.

• Once the site is weed-free, create a fine tilth.

• If you are using grass within your mix, keep it to a minimum (at most 25 per cent) and do not use known aggressive grasses such as Yorkshire fog (*Holcus lanatus*) and cocksfoot (*Dactylis*).

• Some seeds may settle out during transport. Make sure the seed is well mixed before sowing – don't just rely on the standard of the mix in the bag.

• A technique to ensure accurate sowing rates is to section the area into quadrants and divide the seed to suit. Remember, measure twice, sow once. Keep some in reserve as insurance. Once the seed is sown you will not be able to collect it up, so if you get it wrong make sure it is wrong by having seed left over rather than running out!

• Ensure good soil-to-seed contact. Seeds like to be shallow-sown but are then prone to drying out. Use a rake or brush to scuff the seeds into the surface. Lightly roll the area after sowing.

• A ridge roller can help to stabilize the soil, offering protection from wind and heavy rain.

• If you are sowing on a slope be aware of soil migration – seeds can wash to the bottom, leaving bare patches at the top.

• As the seedlings develop, you are provided with the best opportunity for weeding out anything that you don't want. Small weeds are much easier to deal with but can be hard to recognize.

• No fertilizer is required at any stage of ground preparation or sowing wildflowers.

• As seedlings emerge, help them to become well established as quickly as possible by occasional watering if required.

How to sow wildflower seed

1 Sowing wildflowers requires very low seed rates of 2–4 g per m². By comparison, a lawn is sown at 30 g per m². This pinch of seed is enough for 1 metre!

2 To improve the accuracy of sowing, mix the seed into a bulking agent to help achieve an even spread. Scatter by hand on a wind-free day.

3 Using a quadrant, apply a pre-determined amount of seed as evenly as possible. Working backwards, sow half the seed in roughly horizontal lines then turn 90 degrees and repeat.

4 Alternatively, for areas more than a few metres in size, you can use a seed spreader to gain a more accurate distribution, but take care with calibration.

5 Once the seed has been applied, lightly rake the area to mix the seed into the surface of the soil. Keep the raking depth to a maximum of 1 cm (¾ in).

6 Press the surface of the soil by trampling or rolling to seal in moisture and ensure that the seed has good contact with the soil.

7 Use a roller for larger areas to help seal in the moisture and improve the chances of germination.

8 Water well to break seed dormancy. As seedlings emerge, ensure that they are watered from time to time to encourage and maintain growth.

Creating a meadow with turf

The preparation required for turfing a meadow is similar to seeding but there isn't the need to be quite as thorough. The weed control can be done in one go as the turf is instantly competitive once laid. While rotovating is required, the surface doesn't need to be completely level as the thickness of the turf helps to even things out. However, for successful establishment the turf requires soil-to-root contact and so an adequate tilth is still necessary. Having said that, the roots of the turf are amazingly robust and keen to establish themselves.

Wildflower turf is relatively light in comparison to traditional lawn turf, owing to the soil-less growing methods. When laying the turf, the pattern illustrated below is advised for optimum speed and accuracy, but this isn't essential and the turf will quickly root in when laid. Any offcuts will establish if placed on soil, so there should be very little wastage.

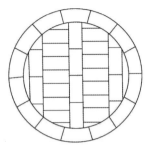

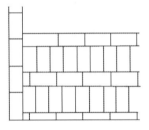

Above: When laying the turf, take care to ensure that all joints are butted up correctly.

Below: Do not overlap the turf at the joints, nor create tension that causes joints to pull apart or shrink.

Laying turf on a slope

Turf can be laid onto slopes with angles of up to 70 degrees. It can prove a little difficult to prepare the soil on a steep slope, particularly with inclement weather as heavy rain can wash soil to the base of the slope, but once laid, turf will be beneficial for soil stabilization.

Lay the turf from the top down, pegging in the top two corners of each turf, usually with wooden pegs that will degrade over time. You can use metal pegs but you will need to take these out once the turf has rooted to avoid later damage to cutting machines.

correct

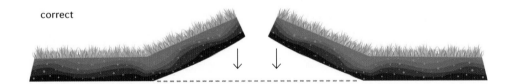

wrong

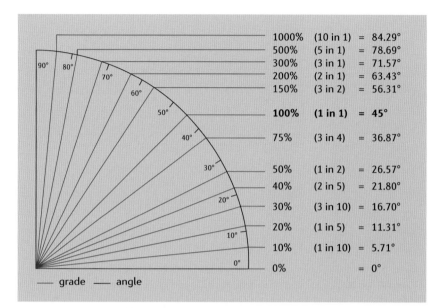

1000%	(10 in 1)	=	84.29°
500%	(5 in 1)	=	78.69°
300%	(3 in 1)	=	71.57°
200%	(2 in 1)	=	63.43°
150%	(3 in 2)	=	56.31°
100%	**(1 in 1)**	**=**	**45°**
75%	(3 in 4)	=	36.87°
50%	(1 in 2)	=	26.57°
40%	(2 in 5)	=	21.80°
30%	(3 in 10)	=	16.70°
20%	(1 in 5)	=	11.31°
10%	(1 in 10)	=	5.71°
0%		=	0°

—— grade —— angle

This chart shows the various ways in which a slope can be described, either as a percentage, an angle in degrees or as vertical change compared to horizontal change. This may help you understand how a slope has been described to you on landscape drawings.

Top tips for turf laying

• If you are using glyphosate to prepare your designated area, give it enough time to work – normally 10–14 days.

• Glyphosate must be applied to a dry leaf on a dry day and 24 hours without rain is required after spraying.

• To improve the speed of establishment, water the prepared soil to saturation point 48 hours before laying the turf.

• The laying of the turf should be reasonably quick – a bowling green finish is not needed!

• It is not essential to work off planks unless the soil is really soft and you find yourself sinking into it.

• A light roller can be applied if the turf has gone down onto particularly uneven ground but is not necessary in normal conditions.

• If you are laying turf around the base of a tree, set it back, so that the turf is not competing with the tree for nutrients and moisture.

This area can be mulched to retain moisture for the tree and keep weeds from establishing.

• Ensure good root-to-soil contact when laying; a good watering will help to achieve this.

• There is no requirement for fertilizer.

• Even tiny pieces of turf will grow well, so there should be very little wastage.

• Ensure the soil is not waterlogged or compacted prior to laying the turf.

How to lay wildflower turf

1 Start by cleaning the area using glyphosate. Apply to a dry leaf on a still day when rain isn't forecast for 24 hours.

2 Dig or rotovate to a depth of 5–15 cm (2–6 in), depending on the level of soil compaction. The intention is to loosen and aerate the soil to allow easy establishment of plant roots.

3 Rake off clods, root material and large stones to leave a level and reasonably fine tilth. Stack the turf near where you are working before laying it.

4 Roll out your turf, pressing it down to ensure good root-to-soil contact. Try to finish laying within 24 hours of delivery.

5 Each turf must butt up to the next without overlapping or leaving gaps. This helps to prevent weeds growing up from beneath the turf.

6 Use a half moon to edge and cut around awkward shapes. A serrated knife can be useful for detailed cuts. Any small off-cuts can be used by patching together.

7 Immediately after laying the turf, water it thoroughly. Check that the soil underneath the turf is damp to be sure you have given it adequate water.

8 Within a few days, pull up a corner of the turf. You should see that the roots have started to establish and knit into the soil.

Creating a meadow with wildflower earth

Preparing your ground for a wildflower-seeded earth installation requires a different approach and is certainly the least labour-intensive. Adding a layer of growing medium that includes the seed means that the receiving area does not need to be prepared to a bare loose soil, however do apply the seeded earth to the correct depth. Bringing in the perfect 25 mm (1 in) of seeded topsoil opens up opportunities that you don't get with conventional seeding techniques. The seed benefits from a ready-made environment that is as good as you can get for germination and establishment. The growing medium is clean of weed seeds and therefore a cure-all to the problems that are dug up with seedbed preparation, ensuring a catalyst for optimum growth.

For the success of this method, it is essential that the existing vegetation on the site is killed off without disturbing what lies below, either by using glyphosate or by stripping the top layer with a turf cutter. The key to preparation is to avoid disturbing the soil surface and therefore breaking the dormancy of the weed seeds that lie within it. The lack of preparation with regard to rotovation and creation of tilth gives this method an advantage as dormant seeds in the ground will not be given so much of an opportunity to germinate. In fact many weed seeds are suppressed under the new layer of wildflower earth, burying them before they wake. Using this method, success is probable – the main threat comes from failing to remove existing plants properly prior to installation or from weed seeds that are blown into the area before the wildflowers germinate.

Top tips for wildflower earth

• The ideal time to start this type of application is from the beginning of March to the end of October.

• While the earth may be applied during the summer, you cannot rely on natural irrigation. If the weather is dry, you can expect to be watering the earth until the seeds have germinated and are well established.

• Glyphosate is the main tool for successful meadow development using this method. If the prepared area does not receive the correct dose or if areas were missed, there is a chance that weeds will reappear through the earth. If you see weeds that are not dying after 7-10 days, reapply glysophate.

• There is no need to rotovate the soil, provided it is not heavily compacted. By not turning over the soil, you will be limiting the opportunity for weed seeds to establish and take over.

• The required depth of application is very important. Less than 25 mm (1 in) will increase the likelihood of weed ingress as well as failing to provide the required seed rate. Over-application has the effect of too much nutrient and a seed rate that is too high, which may limit species diversity in the long run.

• A knobbly roller is a useful tool to have if you are applying the earth to shallow banks. The imprints will reduce slippage caused by heavy wind and rain.

How to establish wildflower earth

1 An accurate coverage of glyphosate is essential for weed control. Apply to a dry leaf, ideally when there is no rain forecast for the next 24 hours. After 10–14 days the plants will be dead.

2 Remove any excess dead grass with a mower or heavy rake to leave the area reasonably clear of dead plant material. There is no need to rotovate or dig the soil, which would encourage weed seeds to germinate.

3 Spread the pre-mixed seeded growing medium to entirely cover the prepared area. For a larger area this can be mechanized.

4 Using a flat edge, such as a scraper or top edge of a rake, disperse the earth to ensure an even depth.

5 The required depth is 25 mm (1 in), which provides good coverage for a weed-suppressing effect and also provides the optimum sowing rate of seed.

6 Ensure that the material is pressed to the soil surface. For smaller areas, heeling in is simple and effective.

7 For larger areas, rolling with a flat or ridged roller will help to prevent the material being blown about. It also improves contact between the seed and growing medium to aid quick germination, helps to lock in moisture and limits damage during heavy rain.

8 In the growing season, you will start to see significant seedling development within 10–14 days.

Getting your meadow established

Seed

If you have seeded your perennial meadow, the first growing season is crucial in the management of the establishing plants. As the seeds germinate and seedlings start to appear you will need to sharpen up on your identification of weeds so that you can have a targeted approach. Hand-pulling should be relatively easy while the weeds are young, but be careful to take out the whole root. Alternatively, using glyphosate is a quick and easy method where it is painted or dabbed onto individual plants and avoids damaging anything else within the area. Weeds will generally be characterized by much quicker growth and some, such as thistles and docks, are reasonably easy to spot once you get your eye in. Avoid any general weed-killers or general spraying as there is no weed-killer available to target individual weeds within the multi-species wildflowers and grasses.

   The other general approach to controlling weeds is regular cutting and removing of material. This has the effect of keeping weeds in check, stopping them seeding. Regular removal of plant material has the added effect of depleting nutrients from the soil. This should start after the seedlings have reached a height where mowing is effective. Aim for the first cut at 5–10 cm (2–4 in); subsequent cuts can be lower than this. You should do a minimum of three cuts during the first year, each time removing the cut vegetation to prevent it smothering the

Hand-pulling weeds is easy and effective in the early stages but can be time-consuming. As the weeds develop, make sure you take out the tap roots of thistles and docks.

wildflowers. Because the wildflowers are perennial they can cope with this regular set back, putting strength into their roots rather than the top growth helps to make them competitive. Many would advise that this first-year cutting should be carried out every two weeks through the entire season, and some say it should be done for the first three years. This will depend on the weed burden of the site, but it obviously limits the visual appeal of the meadow. Throughout the summer be vigilant with weed control.

Identifying weeds

It is particularly difficult to recognize the difference between weeds and wildflowers in the early stages of your sown meadow but it is the best time to take action. If you can identify which are the most likely weeds for your area, it will be a lot easier to get rid of them now rather than leaving it until they are well established. Early action will help to keep weed control achievable. As the weeds grow, they will kill the wildflowers by using their light, moisture and nutrients and if the weeds are allowed to set seed, subsequent control becomes harder. If you are unable to identify all weeds make sure you can at least identify the weeds that are common to your area. For example, my weed archenemies are docks, thistles, nettles, ragwort, cow parsley and fat hen. Get to know these as your enemy and make sure you remove them as soon as you see them.

Below left: An alternative to digging out weeds is painting individual plants with glyphosate. It is an accurate way of chemical removal.

Below right: Spot-spraying with glyphosate is the quickest and easiest method of individual weed control, but be accurate; a gung-ho approach will result in removing plants you do want!

Watering a seeded meadow

To give seeding the best chance of being successful you want to ensure that the seeds establish quickly in order to get them as competitive as possible in as short a time frame as possible. To achieve this, sow in good growing conditions, when there is light, heat and moisture available. If there is a long dry spell after sowing it is worth watering the area on a regular basis. Where the soil is dry, gentle watering is important to ensure optimum growing conditions. Avoid waterlogging, which can not only rot the seed but risks washing it off, leading to patchy areas. The critical time to water is if there is a dry spell after the seedlings emerge. At this stage the plants are small and do not have the capacity to survive a drought period. It is possible to lose a lot of establishing plants at this stage, especially if the soil is south-facing, free-draining and prone to drying out quickly.

Turf

How quickly the roots of your turf go down into the soil will depend on the time of year that it was laid. If there is a little warmth in the soil and moisture is available you can expect that within 1–2 weeks the turf will have taken and you will start to see top growth. Picking up a corner of the turf will allow you to check on how well it is establishing. If it is laid before April you are likely to see the first flowers by May and growth can be quite rapid, reaching 40–50 cm (16–20 in) by the beginning of June.

The early stages of your meadow are likely to be characterized by the more quickly establishing pioneer perennials such as ragged robin, pink campion and oxeye daisy and the growth is vigorous. In following years the meadow will become more diverse as slower establishing species such musk mallow and common toadflax gain strength and develop mature root systems. Years one and two are likely to have robust growth as the established wildflowers in the turf make the most of the nutrients available at their new home. This can be a little daunting but at least you know that there has been good establishment and good establishment is the key to success. Over the years and with the ongoing maintenance this early, robust growth will ease a little to give a more open sward and less plant material to remove at the end of the year.

The character and composition of the meadow will continue to change over time. Eventually a relatively stable community will develop, the balance of which will reflect management, soil fertility and the natural environment of the site.

Watering turf

The need to water wildflower turf will depend on the time of year it is laid. Watering isn't always required, but when it is, doing it correctly is important! Some people think that showing the turf the hose provides sufficient water, while others seem to believe that they need to create a paddy field. Somewhere in between is ideal, but it all depends on conditions at the time.

If the turf is laid in the growing season (March to September) be prepared to water it over the time it takes to get roots established and into the soil to a depth of 5–10 cm (2–4 in). While plants are active and

A garden sprinkler is an ideal way to help newly laid turf through its first summer.

transpiring, it is vital to water the turf if it, or the soil under it, dries out. Sprinklers work well and will only need to be turned on every other day provided they are given enough time to soak through the turf and into the soil underneath. If you measure the water applied, aim for a minimum of 6–7mm (¼ in) per application.

If the turf is damp because of rain or irrigation there is no need to keep watering, nor if it is laid outside the growing season as the plants will be fairly dormant and the roots will gradually work their way into what is likely to be damp soil. In winter conditions, growth will slowly continue while temperatures remain above freezing. Wildflowers are very drought-tolerant and once the turf is established with its roots down deep they will generally look after themselves.

It is possible to overwater the turf. While this will not kill anything, it makes life very easy for the grass and it can quickly dominate as a result. Wildflowers respond well to tough conditions and displays can be excellent in dry years. During a dry spell, grass growth is limited allowing the flowers to take a lead. Having said that, a drought will stress everything and in these conditions, one good soak every two weeks will help extend the flowering time.

Wildflower earth

The speed of establishment of wildflower earth will depend on when it is installed. This can be from early March through to the middle of October, but the prime time is early spring or early autumn. If it is a

In the earliest stages of seed establishment, identify your weeds and pull them out manually.

particularly dry time, water the area intermittently in the same way as for seeding. If preparation has been thorough you are unlikely to see much weed ingress but this is still a seeding process, so if weeds appear, treat them in the same way you would with seed establishing, either spot spraying or hand-weeding.

When applying water, check that the profile of the seeded growing medium is wet through by scratching the surface. Do not be fooled by the top of the material looking wet; it takes a while for the water to soak in, and only by disturbing the surface layer can you check it has had sufficient water. Continue watering until the seedlings have grown to about 2–3 cm (¾–1¼ in). If the material is laid in the early spring or autumn you can expect the rain to do most of the watering. Once it is laid, if rain isn't expected it is worth while soaking the area to get the whole germination process started. If installing in the summer, a more structured watering regime will need to be put in place.

Using fertilizer

The need for fertilizer is rare but shouldn't be entirely ruled out. There have been one or two instances of particularly poor soils where very limited fertility has slowed the development of wildflowers. The resultant sparse and unhappy plants struggle to grow, let alone flower, and a light dose of fertilizer can boost their establishment. It is a myth to say that wildflowers hate any nutrient, whether fertility in the soil or artificial fertilizer – it is just that they don't respond to it as well as grasses and weeds. By fertilizing you give these unwanted species the opportunity to outcompete the wildflowers. If you suspect your site is particularly low in fertility and you can see your meadow looks unhappy, perhaps yellow or slow-growing, a general-purpose lawn fertilizer at a low rate can give it a boost. However, this is an unusual situation and tends to be only on sites where the soil has been tampered with. Examples are the Olympic site where there was a lot of manufactured topsoil or where the topsoil has been stripped to expose a low-nutrient, free-draining subsoil such as gravel.

If you use fertilizer to maintain your lawn, take care not to let it spread onto a neighbouring wildflower meadow. To avoid this, use a push spreader and as you get close to the edge of the meadow, protect the area with a board. If fertilizer goes onto the meadow you will see rapid grass growth which will be detrimental to the wildflowers. You can also use liquid fertilizer for a more accurate application.

Minimizing foot traffic

During the establishment phase all animal and human traffic should be kept to a minimum; if the wildflower patch is in a public area or garden where there are animals you may need to fence off the area to avoid damage. This is particularly important if you have used the seeding method. Good establishment is a massive part of creating a successful wildflower meadow and anything that can be done to help this is well worth while.

Take care when spreading fertilizer on the lawn to avoid overlapping onto the wildflower area. A board or barrier will make sure the two are kept separate.

Above: A wildflower area before fertilizer.

Left: The same area after a low-dosage fertilizer.

Creating a wildflower roof

Wildflower roofs work really well as a way of providing a species-rich environment. They are becoming increasingly popular around the world, used on a multitude of buildings from small to large. They provide a great biodiverse habitat offering a wildlife haven where in the past conventional roofs have provided nothing for fauna or the environment. They help new developments to comply with many green regulations as well as softening and camouflaging the visual impact of a new build. The process can be very simple for small domestic projects.

Top tips for a wildflower roof

• Any building will support a wildflower roof, from bike sheds, garages and extensions to new builds, provided there is enough strength to carry the saturated plants and growing medium. One of our green roofs has a saturated weight of 130kg (286 lb) per 1 sq m (1¼ sq yd).

• When designing your roof, remember that access for maintenance will be required. Also plan for a sufficient water supply.

• The most important thing of all is that the roof is 100 per cent waterproof. Bitumen felt is not good enough, but materials ranging from pond liners to professionally installed single-ply membranes or fibreglass will do the job.

• The substrate needs to be free-draining but able to retain as much moisture as possible. An organic compost is ideal as it drains well but holds enough moisture to sustain wildflowers.

• The depth of the substrate should be a minimum of 100 mm (4 in) unless you can irrigate regularly and thoroughly. At 100mm (4 in) the roof will still dry out and supplementary water will help to keep the plants healthy. A standard wildflower mix can manage with very little water but there will be browning off in a very dry season without irrigation.

• Drainage boards aren't essential but can help to disperse water on a flat roof. They are not required on a pitched roof but any additional reservoir material can help to slow down plant moisture loss.

• Sedum has long been a solution for a green roof as it is very drought-tolerant, but it isn't nearly as biodiverse as wildflowers. To establish your wildflower roof, any of the methods discussed above will work.

• To keep your wildflower roof healthy, species-rich and colourful in a dry spell during the summer, some form of irrigation will be required. If drip irrigation hasn't been fitted at the outset, use a sprinkler or on a new-build flat roof, design in a flood irrigation system.

• The wildflower roof will survive without irrigation once established but is likely to brown off if there is no rain. Rest assured it will green up after a maintenance cut and a spell of wet weather.

• Maintain as any wildflower meadow but be careful not to damage the waterproofing.

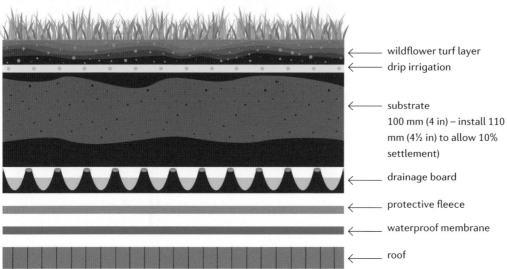

← wildflower turf layer

← drip irrigation

← substrate
100 mm (4 in) – install 110 mm (4½ in) to allow 10% settlement)

← drainage board

← protective fleece

← waterproof membrane

← roof

How to lay turf on a pitched roof

1 Once the roof structure is in place, waterproofing is very important and sealing the edges adequately will help to prolong the lifespan of the roof.

2 Using a filter around the edges will keep loose substrate in place until the roots of the plants stabilize it.

3 On a sloped roof, adding bags of substrate at the edges and apex will ensure that the overall depth is kept to a minimum of 100 mm (4 in).

4 Loose substrate can be applied over the top, using a scraper to provide a fairly level surface. Fill any voids at the corners of the bagged substrate.

5 Drip irrigation can be applied on top of the substrate, with water holes every 300 mm (12 in).

6 Lay the turf directly over the substrate and drip irrigation pipes and press down firmly.

7 Your wildflower roof should perform in exactly the same way as any other meadow, with a wonderful show of flowers from May to August.

8 For an earlier display of colour a green roof can be underplanted with spring bulbs.

Maintaining a meadow

Managing the growth of your perennial meadow with mowing or grazing is essential to the maintenance of its structure, balance and diversity. Without maintenance, grasses would soon dominate reducing biodiversity and interest, and the area would eventually turn into scrub and woodland. No two meadows will grow in exactly the same way or even at the same rate, with the mix of flowers and grasses that flourish varying year on year.

There are a number of different factors that will have a bearing on your meadow. Weather and climate play a big part in the annual growth – in years of early warmth and rain the meadow can reach a height of up to 1 m (3¼ ft) by June. Soil fertility over time can be controlled with the correct maintenance regime, but a fertile site can be expected to have rapid growth in the early years. For this reason a little more maintenance will be required if the meadow is to remain tidy, with a managed appearance. Low-nutrient sites will produce less vegetative growth and therefore less material to remove when cut.

There is considerable scope to vary the pattern of mowing from one spot to another and from one year to the next to create different effects, so don't be scared to experiment to find what suits your site. Perennial wildflowers are extremely hardy once established, so there is little likelihood of permanently damaging the meadow. Experimenting with cutting heights and times is well worth doing as this will help you to recognize the regime that suits your particular meadow and the aesthetic variations that you like.

Tools and machinery

In smaller areas hand tools are easy to use as well as being kind to any animals that might be living among the vegetation, as you can look closely before you cut. Hand shears can effectively cut through stems, whether performing a tidying summer trim or a low-level autumn cut, and are particularly useful around path edges.

Scything is an old method that is seeing a renaissance as it is a zero-carbon alternative to mowing or strimming. It is kinder to plants,

allowing for a cleaner cut rather than shattering the stem. Keeping the blade sharp and the movement horizontal is important to successful scything.

Most landscapers will use a motorized strimmer for speed and accessibility. It is certainly less painstaking than a scythe, but perhaps not so kind for the environment and less rewarding for the gardener. A good-quality motor mower on a high setting or professional mower with a grass collector are often used for managing larger meadows. Do make sure that your blades are very sharp before beginning, particularly if you are cutting in the late summer months onwards; some of the stems will be particularly thick at this stage and you may risk damaging or uprooting the plant if it is not cut sharply. While endless footfall or machinery on the meadow is not ideal, it is acceptable because in the autumn the plants are starting to become dormant ready for the winter and will tolerate traffic. The benefits of a good clear-up of the area far outweigh any risk of damaging the meadow with boots and wheels.

When scything, the blade should always be in constant contact with the ground, even on the return stroke.

A cut in early summer will extend the flowering season and deplete fertility, while reducing the quantity of arisings in autumn. Leave 15-20 cm (6-8 in) to ensure rapid regrowth and a quick return to flowering.

When to mow a meadow

It is best to avoid cutting too often – more than two or three times a year – as this will limit species diversity and the amount of flowers you can enjoy. But treating certain areas within the meadow to different cutting regimes over the years can introduce interesting variations in the areas from one year to the next. The weather will play a significant part in you deciding when is an appropriate time to cut, with drought-like conditions meaning that flowering is likely to occur earlier for all species and the meadow will look scruffier by July. In years of heavy rain, you are likely to see a lot more growth and an earlier cut will avoid the risks of collapsing meadows and dense, matted swards that can be disease- and pest-prone.

With any cut, but particularly early-season cuts, it is a good idea to time them with the prospect of rain or watering soon after. While it is preferable to be handling dry cuttings, the meadow will benefit greatly from a thorough watering after the clippings have been gathered – one really good soak is generally enough. The cut will stress the meadow, so giving it a little help by watering it ensures speedy regrowth and encourages further flowering.

Early spring cut – suitable for grassy meadows

If you are naturalizing a meadow or if mild and wet conditions over winter have led to rapid grass growth, an early cut between March and April will help to control the grasses. Taking the sward back to 2–5 cm (1–2 in) will mean the flowers and grasses have the same starting point for the beginning of the growing season. Do not attempt an early cut if you have underplanted the area with spring bulbs.

Summer cut – suitable for rapidly growing meadows

This late spring or early summer maintenance cut is a bit of a leap of faith as the meadow may well be looking at its best. A strimmer with a hedge-trimmer attachment is the perfect type of tool to use for this cut, taking off the top layer to a height of about 20 cm (8 in). The purpose of the cut is to remove a large proportion of the plant material that is about to finish flowering. By cutting at this height, you will see some flowering buds under the 20 cm (8 in) level and there will be enough vegetation left for flowers to quickly re-establish. You must be quite careful when clearing the cut material from the meadow at this time of year. Using a fork to lift the arisings clear is ideal and raking should be done carefully. With this cut, you will definitely lengthen the flowering period of the meadow and it is a very effective way of depleting nutrients. Another bonus of this two-cut regime is that it makes the final cut in the autumn a lot easier because there will be less material to clear.

Late summer cut – scruffy meadows/drought years

In some people's eyes, senesced growth (browning vegetation and seed heads) can look scruffy, although senesced meadows are enjoyed by many as the plants sway in the breeze and add a seasonal look. A cut at this time of year can tidy up the whole area and will be of great benefit to the late-flowering species within the meadow such as toad flax, mallow, yarrow, vetch and scabious. Around mid-August, take the browning vegetation off to leave about 5 cm (2 in) height. Once you have cleared the cuttings, give the area a really good water. Within days you should see the whole area green up again and some flowers will show in September. You cannot expect a lot of colour, but those later-flowering plants will continue until your final maintenance cut in the autumn.

By late summer the area can start to look scruffy, particularly in a dry year. Consider a cut to tidy up and encourage the late-flowering plants.

In a one-cut regime, by late summer you will have senesced plants, as shown here. Be prepared to remove a lot of material – a short cut to a height of 2-4 cm (1-2 in) and thorough rake off is required.

Final maintenance cut

Whether you have decided to make cuts earlier in the year or not, you will always need to do a final maintenance cut in early to mid-autumn after the wildflowers have set and shed their seed. This cut is essential for the health of the meadow, as not only will it tidy up the area for the winter it will also stop the senesced summer growth from covering the growing plant in a layer of slowly degrading material. If this material isn't removed it will act as a barrier for the regrowth of the parent plant and seedlings and also reintroduce a level of nutrients that is best avoided. An open sward over the winter ensures healthy, disease-free plants which can benefit from what light and warmth is available to them during these months.

If you have not cut the meadow earlier in the year there is likely to be quite a bit of material to remove, depending on soil fertility. A one-cut regime will mean the autumn cut isn't that easy as some stems are tough to get through. Good tools will help. If you find it laborious, remember that you haven't had to do anything else over the year until now! Once it is cleared you will find that your meadow starts to grow again, although how much regrowth will depend on the time of the cut, soil fertility, moisture levels and the weather.

Allowing the meadow a chance for regrowth before it becomes dormant during the colder months is a good idea, if only to have it looking green and healthy over winter. When spring approaches, the wildflowers are in the perfect position to develop quickly and repeat their perennial cycle, thus guaranteeing a wildflower meadow year after year.

Top tips for the final maintenance cut

• When planning your maintenance cut, choose a dry day – you will find the cuttings lighter and easier to clear.

• Be thorough with your clearance of all dead plant material. If left this material will break down and add fertility to the soil. The aim is to exhaust nutrient levels to help the wildflowers remain competitive, and to reduce grasses and nutrient-loving plants such as fat hen and dock weeds. Rotting material left on site will suppress new growth and also be a haven for pests such as slugs.

• When clearing the area with a rake, be thorough and don't be afraid to be a bit rough. This will pull out any thatched material and allow light and air to the roots. The plants are hardy and will not be affected by some tough love. A quick and easy option is to run a rotary mower with collector over the area.

• A staggered cutting programme will help wildlife. Cutting half the area one day and then delaying the second half for a week or two will allow fauna to migrate to the uncut area. By the time of the second cut, the first cut area will have some regrowth to provide a beneficial habitat. Although the cutback seems a bit extreme for wildlife, maintaining the meadow ensures it is there for the long term – it is part of the natural cycle for a wildflower meadow.

• If you compost the cuttings, give them a soak to speed decomposition.

• Be vigilant with leaf and fruit removal after the autumnal cut. It will be much easier to clear fallen leaves once you have cut and removed the summer growth. Do not leave them as a mat of overpowering material. This will crowd out the wildflowers and as it rots, it will add nutrients to the soil and provide a potential risk of disease.

• Observe your meadow from year to year and consider your strategy for the year ahead.

How to make the final autumn cut

1 If you only cut once and haven't done this by the end of September, your meadow will have senesced and will require its annual cut and clearance.

2 Cut your meadow using shears, a strimmer, a hedge cutter (as shown here) or a mower. The aim is to cut as low to the ground as possible, with a cut height of 25–40 mm (1–1¾ in).

3 Remove as much of the cut material as possible, using a fork or rake. Be as thorough as you can.

4 All material should be removed from the meadow to reduce soil nutrient levels.

6 For larger areas there is purpose-built cut-and-collect machinery to do all of this in one pass.

7 These machines are quick and easy and efficiently collect and compact all arisings.

7 The collected material can make excellent compost.

8 There is likely to be regrowth in autumn so aim for the meadow to overwinter at 4–6 cm (1½-2½ in) maximum. A mower with a collector can be used after strimming to tidy the area and achieve the correct cutting height.

Taking care of wildlife

Varying mowing times and the mown areas within the meadow, and rotating these from year to year, is a good way to maintain a diverse and species-rich sward. It is also the kindest way of guaranteeing a healthy and beneficial habitat for wildlife. You can expect to see a range of wildlife when you cut back the meadow, including newts, frogs, slow worms, grass snakes, voles and mice. In the meadow on the edge of our very busy farm road, I came across a pair of partridges with a nest of 12 eggs.

The final maintenance cut is essential to provide the long-term benefit to wildlife that a diverse and species-rich wildflower meadow brings, but try to be sympathetic at cutting time; many animals will have used the protection this habitat provides to hide a nest. However, by the time of the autumn cut the nest is often finished with; this was certainly the case with the partridges, which had hatched and moved on by mid-July so the cut did not affect them. For some, though, it is a more permanent habitat and a cut is disruptive.

In a larger area, cut and remove half the meadow and return to complete the rest 1–2 weeks later as this will enable the vegetation to recover in the cut section and provide a place for wildlife to move into as you remove the second half of the meadow. In larger meadows that provide extensive summer habitat, leave some patches or edges uncut through winter to provide refuge for insects.

While cutting the meadow is disruptive to nature, the wildlife is there because the meadow is providing them with essentials for life. If the meadow is not maintained it will not be there to do this. So although wildlife is disturbed, the cycle is natural, and symbiotic with a long-term benefit for all.

Enhancing a meadow

Whatever stage you have reached with a wildflower space there is always an opportunity to improve it, adding benefit to all concerned. As the meadow-maker, you will find it's great to see things develop because of work you have done over the years and anyone who sees the area will appreciate the care that has gone into it. And of course, all the fauna will love it and use it more and more. So, with all this appreciation coming your way, you will probably feel encouraged to enhance your meadow further. Here are some methods to help.

Patching

Patching with seed is a great technique to add species diversity and can also be used as a remedial action to maintain and improve the meadow. Areas of bare ground provide an opportunity to introduce more wildflowers, either of the same species or new ones. If you don't take this opportunity, nature will! These will either be plants from the seed of your nearby wildflowers, or undesirables that are blown in from a neighbouring weed patch! Nature abhors a vacuum.

It is important to understand why the bare ground is there – the reason could be anything from damage by animals such as moles to waterlogging or excess leaf litter. Providing it isn't an ongoing problem, see the bare ground as an opportunity and give nature a helping hand.

Patching a meadow with seed is inexpensive as you don't need to add a great deal of it – and if you harvest seed from plants that are already established, either nearby or on site, it won't cost anything at all. This doesn't guarantee success but if you find a species that does well locally, then it is likely it will work to fill the hole. Understanding what works through experimentation keeps costs down and limits wasted time and effort trying to establish what won't work.

The perfect time to sow is directly after the seed has been harvested. It stands to reason that if nature is distributing seed, then that is the perfect time for you to do it too. Patch with harvested seed as described on the following pages.

How to harvest seed

1 From July (early varieties) to October (late varieties), wildflowers will set seed and be ready to harvest

2 Collect the seed head from the stem by hand.

3 Different flowers will have different shapes and sizes of seed. Rub out the seed head and collect the seed – it can be hard to distinguish it from the chaff, but provided you haven't left it too late there should be seed there somewhere. If in doubt, use it all.

4 If the seed is contained within a pod you will need to break this open.

How to patch an area

1 Find a bare patch or use shears to clear an area of all green material. A size of about 30 x 30cm (12 x 12 in) works well in order to give the seeds a chance to establish without too much competition.

2 Choose your species – you will need only a few seeds per patch to provide them with the best chance of establishing. An area of 30 x 30 cm (12 x 12 in) would need around 10 seeds.

3 It is important to have good soil-to-seed contact, so press the seed into the soil rather than just scattering it from above.

4 Alternatively, use a pre-seeded growing medium which gives a better chance of germination.

Plugging

Having dealt with a number of sites where plugs have been used as a way of establishing a wildflower meadow, my advice would be to avoid them for this purpose. However, plugging is an excellent way of enhancing an existing wildflower meadow and particularly useful to those who have a botanical interest in their meadow as it is an easy way to include more species than are found in a particular geographical area.

Using plugs also allows you to select individual wildflowers that suit a soil type or location and introduce them as established and instantly competitive plants. While these plants are likely to appear anyway, using plugs ensures a quick take up, rather than having to wait a few years for a natural colonization. With instantly competitive plants you are more likely to have success when introducing them to a specific site; in my experience the bigger the plant, the better the results as they are better equipped to survive. Using smaller, cheaper plants is probably a false economy. You can never be sure that plugs will be effective and so there is no point in spending money on numerous plants – instead, use your money on bigger plants, choosing 4–5 species that particularly interest you. Treat your first foray into plugging as a bit of an experiment as you find out which will or will not succeed.

Both plugging and patching with seed are useful techniques to enhance a meadow and increase species diversity, but neither of them guarantee success and sometimes the results may not be seen for two or three years, if at all. Some species will do better than others and you will not know until you have tried them. It is useful to record what you have done and what the results were so that you can refer back to the results and work out what definitely works in order to improve your meadow year on year.

Bulbs

While there are some early-blooming wildflowers such as campion and cowslip, early spring can be cold and day length is still relatively short, so full colour does not normally get going until mid-May. For many gardeners part of the beauty of a wildflower meadow is its ever-changing natural state, but for others the first few months of the year can seem a bit bereft of colour and interest, particularly in a small garden.

How to plug an area

1 Within the existing meadow, find a site where there isn't too much competition. Dig your hole in preparation to accommodate the size of plug that you are using.

2 Rather than scattering the extracted soil, try to collect it and discard elsewhere in case you have awakened weed seeds that are within it.

3 Place the plug in the prepared hole.

4 Press in firmly and make sure it is well watered.

Planting spring bulbs in swathes creates maximum impact and is best suited to municipal areas, highways being a good example. You can achieve a more natural look simply by using fewer bulbs.

The addition of naturalizing spring bulbs will extend the flowering season of the area. The subtle colour that they can bring among the early green growth of the wildflower plants will be very apparent. The bulbs start flowering before there is any new season growth from the wildflower plants and progress as the rest of the meadow wakes up from winter dormancy. Bulbs can either be added to an established meadow or underplanted when creating the area from scratch. Underplanting is straightforward and there are a variety of techniques that can be adopted according to the establishment method of a new meadow, the size of the area and the look that you would like to create.

For smaller areas, hand planting is advisable, as you can be more prescriptive as to where you are putting the bulbs. A dibber for smaller bulbs or a hand-held planter work well. This method should also be used for green roofs, wielding the tool carefully so as not to damage the waterproof lining. However, if you are creating an area more than

20 sq m (24 sq yd) the hands and knees method may become tiresome.

Using a turf cutter is great for a defined area of bulbs. The depth of turf to be cut can be altered depending on the bulbs that you are planting. The turf is shaved off in a strip and can be simply relaid after distributing the bulbs on the exposed soil.

For larger areas of wildflower you may want to consider using a specialist bulb planting machine that picks up the turf, plants the bulb and rolls it back over the bulbs. This is a method that makes life easy, but it will require a specialist contractor and uses a high planting rate of over 200 bulbs per square metre (1¼ sq yd). It is expensive and will leave a dense mass of regimented flowers.

If you are creating a wildflower area with turf, it couldn't be simpler, as you can scatter the bulbs directly onto your prepared site and simply lay the wildflower turf over the top. The bulbs then grow through the turf in the spring.

With regard to choosing your bulbs, there are no rules except to avoid oversized foliage bulbs such as daffodils and tulips as they take a long time to become swamped by the developing wildflowers when the bulbs have finished flowering. For a wilder look bluebells, snowdrops, puschkinia and chionodoxa would work well; for big colour impact wild narcissi and crocus fit the bill. Favourites of mine are fritillaria, *Iris reticulata* and scilla; these offer an early source of pollen for bees, whilst maintaining a natural look within the meadow. Summer bulbs can also offer a wonderful juxtaposition in design. Using large-headed, statuesque allium, liatris or eremurus is very effective as they give height and movement among the more fragile wildflowers.

With regard to the depth of planting, the smaller bulbs are certainly easier to handle and cause least disruption to the area. Larger bulbs can be broken if you are rolling turf back on top. Much depends on the look you want to create when it comes to planting density, but I recommend around 20–40 bulbs per square metre (1¼ sq yd) to maintain a natural effect – any denser and you will lose the 'wild' feel of the area. This density may sound a lot, but different species in the mix will flower at different times in the spring, so you won't have this number of flowers at any one time.

With regard to maintenance, your wildflower area does not need to be mown until much later in the summer. Choosing bulbs that have little residual growth after flowering and stems of 20 cm (8 in) or less will mean that by May they will be superseded by the wildflowers and

Above: Choosing summer-flowering bulbs adds height and colour to the meadow in midsummer.

Right: Regular mowing of a path or meadow boundary will give contrast to the wild area and help to prevent grass spreading into the meadow.

will not have any visual impact on the area after this time. If you plant summer bulbs an early-spring cut is obviously not advised.

While incorporating bulbs compromises the native element of your wildflower landscape, underplanting the area with spring bulbs certainly lengthens the season of colour and interest and provides an early nectar source for pollinators.

Paths and mown edges

Pathways running through a meadow area are not only aesthetically pleasing and inviting, but also very practical for navigating through an area that would otherwise be hard to access without trampling over flowering plants and disturbing wildlife. Paths can be mown in at any time, with straight lines or meandering curves, in a design that complements other aspects of your garden or site.

Mown paths and edges define the wildflower space and this contrast between the clipped area and the wild area will enhance the meadow, helping everyone to understand its shape and purpose.

Below: Paths in a wildflower meadow allow you to experience the meadow at close quarters and augment the visual appeal of the meadow.

Above: Wildflowers are the perfect backdrop for this bronze sculpture of hares boxing.

Opposite top left: Include a seat in the meadow so that you can enjoy the peace and tranquillity a wildflower area brings with it.

Opposite top right: Signposting the flora and fauna in a wildflower meadow gives a greater understanding of the benefits of this habitat. This information can make the difference between the meadow's success and failure. Going from lawn to a wild and sometimes 'tatty' meadow requires a change in mindset and interpretation boards help to draw people in.

Opposite right: Using a path or border, either paved or mown, will help to show off a statue, structure or feature in the wildflower meadow.

Sculpture, topiary and trees

The rigidity of a sculpture is beautifully offset by a frame of wildflowers surrounding it, and many garden designers use wildflowers in this way. Even within a small setting, a piece of artwork can totally transform a simple meadow area; it is a wonderful way to enhance a space. Trees and topiary will have a similar effect when set within wildflowers.

The key thing to remember when you place any structure, shrub or tree in a wildflower area is that you will need access. Maintenance will be required at some point throughout the year, whether it is to clean the area of leaves, mulch a planted tree or cut back a topiary shape. I strongly advise that you always leave an area around the structure for access – a 1 m (3¼ ft) margin usually works quite well. This could be mulch, gravel or simply a mown area and it will help to make the tree or sculpture stand out. If you have a number of leaf-shedding trees in your meadow area, you must be vigilant with regard to picking up leaf and fruit litter in the autumn.

Seating areas

One of the exquisite benefits of a wildflower space is the sense of well-being that coming closer to nature can instil. Incorporating a seating area is a lovely way to enhance the area and allow you to enjoy the wildlife that will inhabit the meadow. Make the seat accessible and comfortable and find the time to sit and relax!

Interpretation boards

Wildflower meadows provide excellent learning opportunities and much has been done to create them in educational environments. There are now many more designated wildflower areas within public green spaces and interpretation boards are a great way to raise awareness of the species diversity within them, encouraging visitors to look more closely and identify particular flowers and wildlife. There is an obvious correlation between generating public interest in a meadow and the way in which it is enjoyed and respected by the people that use it.

Solving problems

Wildflower meadows are a long way from the most labour-intensive form of planting, but there will inevitably be some problems to deal with. Most are best solved by early intervention before they get out of hand.

Abundance of weeds

If there is a heavy weed seed burden in the soil or there has been inadequate site planning and ground preparation before installation, you may experience problems with perennial weeds such as thistles, docks and nettles. These can either be weeded out by hand or spot-treated with a herbicide. While many people will want to avoid chemicals, their judicious use as spot applications can make the operation of weeding a much less onerous task and this may make the difference between success and failure for you and the pollinators! Hijacking the weeds as they appear in early spring is the best way to tackle them, since stepping over low growth and taking out small plants is far preferable to battling through mature plants to root out stubborn and well-anchored plants later in the season.

   If these weeds do get the better of you, it is worth while cutting off any seed heads before they become ripe and shed in the summer.

Take action on weeds in early spring as soon as they emerge. Left, young dock and right, emerging groundsel.

At this stage, leave the parent plant to the autumn cut back and then have another go at it the following spring – earlier this time! Limiting the seeding of unwanted plants is relatively easy to do and will help considerably.

Pest control

Your meadow, whether as seed, seedlings or established vegetation, is always likely to offer a tasty treat for many different forms of wildlife. While this is part of the intention, it is best avoided while the meadow establishes initially. Certain pests can devastate areas quite quickly and as soon as you spot the culprit, action should be taken with an appropriate control method. I am not going to prescribe which methods of pest control are the most appropriate as there are numerous options, ranging from chemical to organic control, but understanding the damage caused by each type of pest is helpful in identifying them and dealing with them quickly. Once the plants are well established, the risk of failure is very low.

Slugs love to eat out the middle of larger seeds before they get a chance to germinate. Seedlings are a favourite of flea beetles, some of which will snip the stalk of a seeding like felling a tree, while others will eat the emerging leaves in a way that leaves them looking as if they have been blasted with shot. And slugs will just eat the lot, although initial damage leaves foliage looking as if it has been through a paper shredder.

Birds such as sparrows and pigeons will pick up seeds and pull up seedlings as a tasty snack and small mammals such as rabbits

Below left: Young thistle.

Below: This well-established dock weed should be dealt with before it reaches maturity and the seeding stage. If it is allowed to set seed, one year's seeding means seven years weeding!

Top: Slugs and snail damage can make a serious dent in the plant population during seedling emergence. Once established and growing conditions are favourable the plants will outgrow the damage. Growing a wide range of species helps limit the problem as not all plants will be palatable.

Above: Molehills will damage mowers and quickly introduce weeds if left untended, as weed seeds in the soil turned over by the moles are given perfect growing conditions to germinate and establish.

are capable of tugging out entire plants. If these larger animals are a problem the area should be netted over until the plants are well established. And while it is a nice idea to let your chickens peck around in a meadow, they are devastating, even to mature well-established plants. Badgers and deer can be destructive and if you know that you have a sizable population in the area, you may need to temporarily enclose the area with an electric fence that will deter them until your meadow is fully established. Badgers in particular like bulbs and if you have underplanted your meadow, you may be providing a fast-food outlet for the resident population.

Moles can make an appearance, and while they are only interested in the worms in the soil, the excavation of exposed topsoil is likely to bring on weed development. Once the wildflowers have grown up it is quite difficult to know where the molehills lie. For this reason it is best to remove the excavated soil and then cut the meadow tight (2–5 cm or 1–2 in) at the end of autumn or early spring and rake down the mound of earth and fill with seed. If molehills are prolific and left untreated, your meadow will start to look patchy as pockets of plants are uprooted over time and weed ingress will be swift on the exposed soil. Rolling the area will compact the ground and deter the moles; trapping can be used if the problem escalates.

Disease

Fortunately, disease in the form of fungal attack is very rare in wildflower meadows. The more pampered grasses, especially the cultivated grasses found in lawns and pitches, are prone to all sorts of problems from red thread to powdery mildew, brown rust and fusarium, but wildflowers have evolved over time to be resistant to disease. This is due to the diversity of species making it hard for diseases to establish and spread. This is the opposite of the monoculture of a cropped species where fungal disease can take hold and, given suitable conditions, will spread at such speed as to devastate a crop if fungicides are not applied.

Grass-dominated wildflower meadows

One of the biggest problems with establishing and preserving a wildflower meadow is when grasses take over and crowd out the less competitive wild flowers.

The underlying issue is that grasses are vigorous, especially in a temperate climate, where they have good growing conditions throughout the year. In an area that is pampered, they are the quickest plants to respond and they can soon dominate. Feeding and watering will result in a very healthy grass sward. Wildflowers are the opposite. Once they have established, they respond well to harsh conditions. They don't need fertile soils (they will grow in fertile soil, but weeds and grasses will grow quicker and stronger), they are very drought-tolerant and they cope very well with really cold spells (as seen in alpine meadows).

So don't feed a wildflower meadow and there is no need to water it either apart from while it is establishing – and even then, give it only enough water to stop the emerging plants from wilting. There is no controlling the temperature and the UK is a temperate climate so winters can be relatively mild, especially in the south. During the winter all plant growth slows and wildflowers will become dormant. In a mild winter, however, grasses will continue to grow and it is then that they can get away and outcompete the wildflowers.

There are a number of ways to help the wildflowers, though. While it is healthy to have some grass in the meadow, when you are establishing it, use very little grass seed and ensure that the grass species used are slow and low-growing. However, it is likely there is less desirable grass seed already in the soil and it will find its way into the meadow one way or another. It is easy to add grass but very difficult to take it out.

If the grass does become dominant, the main method to control it is to cut the meadow and remove the cut material. This should be done regularly, 4–10 times in the growing season, depending on how much grass there is. Cutting it before it sets seed is also important. This regular cutting will deplete the soil nutrients and help the wildflowers to get established and while it will limit the flowers, a sward dominated by grass will give very little, if any, flowers and colour. So the cut is important and a good clearing technique is vital. After the cut a heavy rake will make a big difference, and while it will stress the area in the short term, it will be very beneficial in the longer term.

There is a lot of talk of yellow rattle (*Rhinanthus minor*) being the silver bullet for grass control as it is parasitic on grass and its roots. This is true and it is a lovely wildflower to have in a meadow, but for every success story I hear, there is another story that goes 'We tried yellow rattle seed and couldn't get it to germinate.' It is definitely

Three strands of temporary electric fence, placed low to the ground, will deter badgers. Make sure you keep the fence from being earthed by twigs, weeds and grasses as this will leave it ineffective.

Top: Grass dominance in a meadow will affect the diversity of species and subsequent number of flowers through the season.

Middle and above: Adding yellow rattle to your meadow helps to control the grasses.

worth having it in a seed mix, or adding it to your meadow in the form of a plug plant as a solution when the grass is strong. Once the yellow rattle is properly established, it can dominate the area at the expense of other wildflowers. If this does happen, cutting it before the seed sheds will help to control it.

There are a couple of chemical options too. Using glyphosate sounds radical, but it can work if it is applied very carefully, to the grass only. Each grass plant only needs a drop of chemical and it will succumb. Using a paintbrush is time-consuming but accurate.

The alternative option for larger meadows is a chemical that specifically kills grass only. While it is chemical control and will not suit everyone, it can be very effective and may be the difference between success and failure. These chemicals will have to be applied by a professional agronomist who will advise on the correct chemicals to use.

Ox-eye daisy and single species domination

One of the taller wildflowers, the ox-eye daisy is reliable and quick to establish. Once they start flowering in mid to late June, they are particularly noticeable and can visually overwhelm the other species. If you were to conduct a species survey of your meadow you would definitely find other species throughout it, but the ox-eye can look dominant so that less obvious flowers can go unnoticed for at least 2–3 weeks in June and July.

Ox-eye domination is especially prevalent in newly created meadows – this plant is often described as an early colonizer and its growth can be fairly thuggish in the first few years. It is easy to forget that you may well have had a month of other beautiful wildflowers and once the ox-eyes have died back you will then have a whole host of late-flowering wildflowers visible such as scabious, knapweed, yarrow, wild carrot and toadflax.

Many people, including me, love the cheerful and vibrant look of the daisies but if you are really opposed to them you can limit the production of seed by doing a maintenance cut in the first three weeks of June, cutting your meadow down to about 15–20 cm (6–8 in). If you take off the big flush of daisy heads, you should reduce the overall number. Cut with a hedge trimmer rather than a strimmer to avoid shattering the stems completely, then use a long-pronged fork or wire rake to lift the cut foliage away. Cutting at this height will leave plenty of vegetation to produce the energy to provide more flowers later on in the season; any plants that haven't already set seed are liable to throw up flowers again. The added advantages of taking off vegetation at this stage is a quicker depletion of nutrients in the meadow and less material to cut and remove in the autumn.

If you have a fertile site, after 3–4 years of a robust cut and remove maintenance regime you will deplete soil fertility. A more delicate balance of wildflowers will spread and the early dominance of ox-eye will abate. The downside to thinning out the show of ox-eyes is probably an emotional one; just as your meadow looks flush with flowers you will have to take the decision to cut it down and for some people this will be very difficult. But there will be a quick return to a full and more diverse range of wildflowers – you need only compromise the look of your meadow for 2–3 weeks; try it once in a given area and then decide on your preferred approach.

Above: A dense and matted sward such as this needs to be cut back immediately.

Below: Ox-eye domination

Excessive growth combined with heavy rain has left this poppy meadow in a sorry state.

In the same way, other species can appear to dominate a meadow. If this is happening, try to establish if it really is at the expense of all other species or if the dominance is just for a certain time in the season. Either way, consider cutting back before the abundance of seed from the dominant flower is allowed to set and shed and this will help to limit them the following year. I have seen this with yellow rattle, to the extent that there are very few different flowers for the rest of the year. However, because yellow rattle is an annual, cutting it as it flowers and before it seeds is a great way of controlling it. It will not wipe the species out, but will give a chance for other flowers to make an appearance.

A collapsed or flattened meadow

If the growth of your meadow is very lush due to fertile soil and conducive weather conditions in the early growing season, there is a danger of it collapsing and going flat, particularly after heavy rain and strong winds. This is more likely with young meadows in their first few years of development, as soil fertility is likely to be higher until the first few cut and removes. If this occurs an immediate cutback is advisable as this will remove fertile growth (and therefore inherent fertility) and the subsequent regrowth is likely to be much less robust. If the problem persists year on year, it is worth following a two-cut regime as the early cut will help to produce a later-flowering meadow that is shorter, more open and less prone to collapse. In time, as soil fertility drops, the flattened meadow becomes less and less of an issue.

Leaf litter

If your meadow lies under or close to trees, leaf fall in the autumn will certainly be an issue year on year. It is essential that you are vigilant with leaf clearance every autumn. Aim to cut the meadow back before the main leaf fall as this will make leaf-litter clearance much easier. Mowing over the area with a collector is a quick and easy method of leaf clearance, or for smaller areas, sweeping with a besom brush has an added advantage of providing a little aeration to the plants.

Even small piles of leaves left in autumn are likely to create patchy areas of meadow the following year.

While there is no need to be out there collecting leaves as they fall, it is best to do so before they start to break down and rot – it is easier to achieve before they get too waterlogged and once they start to break down most of their nutrient value will have already been transferred to the soil. The odd leaf won't matter but it is important to avoid a blanket of leaf litter as this will crowd out and kill the wildflowers. The nutrient value of this layer will also affect the fertility of the soil and therefore the balance of the meadow. Shade is often blamed for the failure of plants under tree, but as a rule, shade and leaf litter go hand in hand and the latter is far more damaging than partial light or medium shade.

Wear and tear

Wildflower meadows are not ideal for use as a lawn or pitch. While the plants will take some wear and it is fine to occasionally walk on and through the meadow over winter, as soon as the wildflowers start to grow and think about flowering, the area is best avoided. This will help to give the best display of flowers and will also leave the wildlife in peace. So the initial design of the meadow is important and ideally, pathways and desire lines will have been thought about. If you end up with a trampled path as a desire line, it makes sense to create a pathway and one can easily be mown into the meadow. This will help to minimize unnecessary traffic and damage to a much greater area of the meadow. In public areas, signage can help people to understand what is wanted and once the meadow is established, mown edges to define areas as well as interpretation boards will go some way to help keep people off the meadow. Repairing worn-out areas can be done using any of the establishment methods previously described, but if wear is ongoing, sowing a hard-wearing grass is likely to be easier than repeated maintenance to a worn out area.

Waterlogging

Perennial wildflowers will withstand a certain amount of standing water, but if their roots are submerged for weeks at a time remedial action is likely to be necessary. The symptoms of waterlogging tend to be sickly plants and a limited species diversity with only some of the hardiest grasses persisting. If the waterlogging is simply due to exceptional weather, it is likely that the wildflowers will return. Once the area has drained, depending on the time of year, you may have a muddy thatch of material to deal with. Remove this straight away, cut the meadow back to 5 cm (2 in) and allow it to start again. There may be weed ingress or bare patches where plants just haven't been able to cope and remedial patching work will be required. Giving the area a boost with some additional seed may speed their reappearance.

If waterlogging is a regular occurrence, draining the area will sort the problem out; this can be done by hiring a contractor to install some land drains. If the area is permanently waterlogged, having a wetland meadow or a pond may be the answer, using aquatic or marginal plants. There are wildflowers that thrive in slightly damp conditions but there is a difference between damp and waterlogged. Examples of wildflowers known to perform well in wet conditions include creeping buttercup (*Ranunculus repens*), meadow buttercup (*Ranunculus acris*), yellow flag iris (*Iris pseudacorus*), ragged robin (*Lychnis floscuculi*), devil's-bit scabious (*Succisa pratensis*), marsh marigold (*Caltha palustris*), common fleabane (*Pulicaria dysenterica*) and red campion (*Silene dioica*).

Left: The bank is being used as a shortcut to the other side. Creating a single pathway through will prevent damage all along the bank.

Below: Creeping buttercup, meadow buttercup, yellow flag iris, ragged robin, devil's-bit scabious, marsh marigold, common fleabane and red campion are well suited to wet conditions.

PART THREE
Case studies

Starting from scratch

In the last few years there has been a resurgence of interest in wildflower meadows. Various initiatives have encouraged people to create their own, from free seed packs on magazine covers to television shows giving advice on wildlife gardening. Unless an established meadow is resurrected, most of these meadows will be developed in areas that haven't had many, if any, wildflowers in the past. The case studies here look at newly created meadows that have been developed as part of this gardening evolution. These sites are a blank canvas and show how easy it can be to create wildflower meadows in all sorts of locations as long as you follow the key principles of planning and site preparation.

The key to a successful meadow is establishing a healthy and robust wildflower plant community, so choosing reliable techniques is essential.

Front garden

A neglected front garden is brought to life with perennial wildflowers

LOCATION Edinburgh, Scotland.
PURPOSE To create a low-maintenance but striking wildflower area.
INSTALLATION METHOD Native perennial wildflower turf.
SPECIFIC CHALLENGES Creating an area suitable for wildflowers from a concrete driveway.
AREA 75 sq m (90 sq yd).

This front garden was in need of an overhaul, having been a concrete parking space. The owners decided that they wanted to give their house 'kerb appeal' with this landscaping project. A new stone wall had been designed to be in keeping with the surrounding rural architecture and raised beds were built to contain ornamental trees and wildflowers. In view of the cost and work involved in constructing the wall, the owners wanted a quick, simple, high-impact solution for the planting scheme and decided to opt for wildflower turf.

Installation

The previous concrete base meant there was little in the way of topsoil, so the owners brought in a free-draining, low-nutrient, 'as dug' topsoil. The quality of this new soil was unknown, so turf was used to stop any weed seeds from establishing. The soil was given a couple of weeks to settle before the turf was laid over the top. During this time four ornamental trees were planted in the area.

JAMES SAYS . . .

While it is a small site, wildflowers instantly enhanced the rustic stone wall and gave the impression that the garden had always been there. As it is a front garden it is worth keeping a closer eye on the maintenance of the meadow and the cutting regime. An earlier mow in the growing season may be required to stop the wildflowers looking unruly. There are further opportunities to enhance the meadow with bulbs to add interest earlier in the year. The trees will also need monitoring as they are growing in a relatively small space. The canopy should be kept high to avoid too much shade and the owners should also be vigilant with the clearance of leaf litter in the autumn.

Success of the wildflower meadow

The front garden had an open aspect and with regular watering the turf established within a couple of weeks. The first-year growth was much greater than expected, possibly due to the soil having higher fertility than anticipated.

Newly added topsoil runs the risk of having a weed seed burden. Using turf provides established plants, so there is little chance for the weeds to germinate.

Levelling the new soil does not have to be perfect as the textured nature of the wildflower turf immediately disguises any imperfections. When importing this amount of soil, do allow time for it to settle before planting.

Using wildflowers against this newly built wall provides an instant rustic charm and makes the area look as if it has been established for years.

New-build home

Blending a new-build home into its rural surroundings

LOCATION Countryside setting.
PURPOSE To create an instant wild garden from bare soil.
INSTALLATION METHOD Wildflower earth.
SPECIFIC CHALLENGES A new-build project requiring an instant effect.
AREA 500 sq m (598 sq yd).

A set of old cowsheds was converted to provide a new home for a family steeped in farming traditions. It was set on the margins of an arable field and being true guardians of their rural landscape, the family wanted to create a biodiverse environment that would benefit wildlife, provide a low-maintenance garden and blend the new building into the natural surroundings.

Installation

The area had previously been part of an arable field, known not to have a heavy weed seed burden or high soil fertility. The soil around the house was worked with agricultural machinery to form a smooth slope around 180 degrees of the house with a south and south-westerly aspect. Soil was used from the footings and redistributed in order to get the soil levels right. This was left to settle over the winter and glyphosate was used to clean up any weed seedlings prior to the installation. Wildflower earth was applied on top of the soil at a depth of 25 mm (1 in). This layer of wildflower earth was then rolled with an indented packer roller to firm the growing medium and press it into the soil. This technique helps to stop the movement of the medium in the case of strong wind or rain.

JAMES SAYS . . .

It is astonishing how wildflowers can completely transform a landscape. This meadow has successfully blended a new building into the countryside and provided an instant species-rich wildflower garden. While the owners have been very happy with the results, at times they have questioned some species dominance seen over the last five years. There have been particular years where the meadow has appeared to be a blanket of ox-eye daisy, yarrow or wild carrot. However, revisiting the site through the seasons and over the years, it has been interesting to monitor the ebb and flow of particular flowers and five years on there is still a substantial variety of species.

At certain times of year the meadow became a rather dominant feature of the site and to overcome this a series of paths has been cut into the area. In addition, by mowing certain areas immediately around the house once a month, the owners now have a small species-rich lawn against the house. The general feel of the meadow as it is today is less overpowering, inviting regular access and much admiration.

Success of the wildflower meadow

This garden went from bare patch to fully established perennial wildflower meadow in 12 weeks. The success can be attributed to a number of factors that are particularly meaningful when embarking on a seeded meadow project. The site preparation was very thorough and the use of specialist machinery helped to improve soil structure. Particular attention was paid to the cleanliness of the soil and this has a definite impact on allowing the wildflower plants to develop with limited interference from weeds or competitive grasses. The soil was also particularly suitable for wildflowers, being low in fertility. The wildflower earth encouraged the area to grow robustly in the first two years, requiring an early maintenance cut to keep fertility levels stable. By year three the amount of growth had slowed down and the meadow has been very successful in providing an enriched habitat for pollinators, mammals and birds. The owners now enjoy a beautiful meadow and regularly meander through its paths.

Specialist machinery was brought in to prepare the site.

Right: The chalk subsoil was covered with a thin layer of soil and a top dressing of wildflower earth, a pre-seeded growing medium.

Below: A packer roller leaves a dimpled impression to protect against wind and rain displacement of seed and soil.

Above: Midsummer, the summer following the autumn installation of wildflower earth.

Right: Five years later there is incredible species diversity.

From lawn to meadow

Native and non-native wildflowers with spring bulbs for early colour

LOCATION Suburban garden.
PURPOSE To turn the existing lawn into a wildflower area.
INSTALLATION METHOD Wildflower turf.
SPECIFIC CHALLENGES Creating an area of interest in a large expanse of lawn.
AREA 500 sq m (598 sq yd).

The owners had wanted to soften the perimeter of their garden and reduce the amount of mowing needed, while adding more visual appeal with a wildflower meadow. They tried naturalizing an area by leaving established grasses to grow long and introducing a number of plug plants. After two years, they decided that they were not achieving the species diversity or aesthetic results that they wanted. Their local contractor, Souren Ala, was called to help. He wanted to provide them with as much impact as quickly as possible and so used a wildflower turf, established with native and non-native wildflowers. He added a vibrant mix of spring bulbs for extra colour early in the spring. There were also existing areas of daffodils that the client wanted to keep.

Installation

A late installation meant that wet weather impaired the effectiveness of the glyphosate, leaving areas of grass that were not completely killed off. A heavy-duty machine was used to rotovate the area which was then worked with a heavy rake to take away remaining grass and roots. To ease the workload, Souren used a motorized wheelbarrow to transport the turf the distance from the delivery point to the laying area. He decided to use boards to lay the turf as he felt this would perfect the finish.

JAMES SAYS . . .

This was a really interesting project and one where we learnt a lot about daffodils! The problem is that they are a bit thuggish and grow so much more than the meadow in late winter or early spring. While they add early season colour they take a long time to disappear once they have finished flowering. In a lawn, daffodils work well as once they have flowered and had a short time to replenish their bulbs they can be cut down and the area returns to a regularly mown lawn. In a meadow, there isn't the opportunity to easily cut them down so they may linger in an increasingly unsightly state until the spring growth of the meadow (around mid-May) hides them.

If you are keen to maintain existing daffodils within your meadow when using wildflower turf, a late summer or early autumn installation will mean the roots have a stronger hold in the soil and the daffodils will either push through the turf or be suppressed by it. To get over the die-back stage, they can be cut using shears so they don't outstay their welcome.

Success of the wildflower meadow

The turf was laid in November, which is a good time for installation as no watering is required and the turf can establish well while there is moisture in the soil – but no one anticipated the impact the timing would have on this particular site! Souren was called back by the client in February as the existing clumps of daffodils were growing and were unable to break through the turf. While the turf roots had grown into the soil, the early-winter installation meant they weren't in deep enough to stop the emerging daffodils from pushing up the turf. All around the site, small mounds had developed.

In the end, the turf was cut around these mounds to let the daffodils grow through. This remedial action was effective and there was a good show of colour from the spring bulbs. The turf then flowered well in its first season. The owners decided that they prefer a slightly managed look to a really wild appearance, so Souren recommended the use of a two-cut regime, the first at the end of June to about 20 cm (8 in) and the second to ground level much later in the year, around early to mid-October. For the June cut Souren used a petrol-powered hedge trimmer and raked off the clippings, trying to keep any trampling of plants to a minimum. The clippings were used for compost. The owners were delighted with the results but felt they would like to be able to walk through the meadow for a more immersive experience. There is also a large tree to the back of the plot where they wanted to add a swing for their grandchildren, so a meandering 1.5 m (5 ft) wide path was mown in the spring.

LANDSCAPER'S VIEW

Souren notes that some clients want to see results as soon as the flowering season is underway but many of the beneficial plants for wildlife, and specifically pollinators, may not be the prettiest. Souren is going to learn how to use a scythe as he feels it is a great thing to offer clients who like the idea of an entirely traditional wildflower area. It will greatly cut down on noise pollution from motorized machinery and is sympathetic to the local fauna. With later projects Souren has been less cautious when laying the turf and feels it is not necessary to use boards as a meadow does not require quite such a manicured finish as a lawn.

A rotovator is a useful tool on such a large area when preparing a site for turf.

Above: Planting low-growing bulbs under turf is a quick and easy way to bring early spring colour to your meadow.

Left: Existing clumps of daffodils in the soil can be problematic when establishing meadows using turf, depending on the time of year.

Right: Using wildflowers on the perimeter of a large lawn is a great way to add another dimension to your garden and soften the edges.

Urban regeneration

Transforming urban wasteland from scratch

LOCATION Manor Field Park, Sheffield
PURPOSE To redefine wasteland to desirable residential plots for private development and amenity.
INSTALLATION METHOD Seeding.
SPECIFIC CHALLENGES Such a large site had a variety of underlying conditions.
AREA 22 ha (54 acres)

This area of Sheffield had been a neglected landscape for a very long time and the surrounding housing estate, often described as the worst estate in Britain, had high rates of poverty, unemployment and crime. This was a huge project to undertake and in some areas civil engineering was required to take the site back to a workable landscape, mining having been a key component of the area. Funding came from a variety of sources and it was hoped that the introduction of a pictorial landscape would change perceptions of the area while also encouraging investment in housing development. The project was funded by a series of collaborative grants to improve the area over time.

Installation

Seeding was chosen as a very cost-effective method of establishing the landscape and allowed for the testing and introduction of high-impact non-native perennial meadow species. Where there were areas of high fertility, annuals could be used as they thrive on fertile soils. In time, annuals reduce fertility levels, paving the way for a more permanent perennial meadow. Areas of land were sectioned off and planted using a seeding approach with ornamental mixes and amenity grass to be sown all at the same time. Seeding also meant that the land owner was more able to eliminate losses to vandalism – the area suffered significant anti-social behaviour and it was hoped that the new landscape would deter vandals.

The initial scheme covered 4 ha (10 acres) and was made up of low- and high-fertility soils, dry and wet areas and open and shady sites. The ground had to be completely cleared of debris, including 70 burnt-out cars. Seed beds were established and hand-sown as large island beds separated by grass access paths. The meadow areas required three cuts during the first growing season to strengthen the plants and keep the weeds in check. This took place in June, at the end of July and at the end of the season. Weed control involved both spot-spraying and pulling weeds by hand.

Success of the wildflower meadow

While a great deal of work went into the first year after sowing, the sward establishment was very good and has subsequently improved year on year. The meadow is in its twelfth year at the time of writing and is seen as a stunning high-impact landscape. Ongoing management includes one winter burn or spring targeted herbicide spray and one late autumn cut and collect a year. The meadow starts flowering in early spring and continues through to late autumn. It is very attractive to both wildlife and the people in the area and the improved landscapes continue to grow by approximately 1 ha (2½ acres) each year. In 2015, Green Flag status was awarded to this park with its unique meadow planting and low-input management.

JAMES SAYS . . .

This is a great example of seeding working really well. It does show how important preparation and ongoing management is, but if this is done well, the results are outstanding and long term. As is the case with all wildflower areas, getting off to a good start is vital and the attention to detail has paid dividends. What is so unusual with this project is the scale on which it has been achieved and how its success has led to a change in mindset by those living near the park. Instead of an unloved wasteland, the investment in colour and biodiversity has paved the way for a caring and engaged attitude towards the park.

Extensive clearance work was required to allow for preparation of the soil.

After seeding with non-native perennial species, a thorough maintenance schedule was put in place to give the flowers the best chance of establishment.

The long-term colour and diversity has had a transformational effect on the park
and local residents who now see the area as theirs to enjoy and look after.

Creative design

The design of green space, whether private or publicly owned, is more and more important as less and less of it is available. Incorporating wildflowers is very popular in a range of environments from gardens to parks. Here are some examples of how wildflowers can be used to benefit an area in a way that enhances the living space while getting the most from wild and natural planting. Well-designed gardens and landscapes can create high-performance, low-maintenance areas. They really don't have to be large and by altering the maintenance regimes you can even manage the flowering times.

Look upon a wildflower meadow as an opportunity for some creativity within your area, rather than just a patch left for the purpose of biodiversity. These next case studies show unusual and interesting designs which still provide great wildlife habitats, demonstrating there is more to garden design than traditional plant beds.

Modern techniques for establishing a wildflower meadow combined with an exciting design can transform a garden.

University campus

Colourful annuals enliven the landscapes of academia

LOCATION A number of university campuses in the UK.
PURPOSE To provide creative transformations of landscapes in the grounds of learning institutions.
INSTALLATION METHOD Annual seeding.
SPECIFIC CHALLENGES Arranging flowering times to coincide with important dates in the academic calendar.

University campuses have traditionally been maintained to a high standard, as they often have a better level of funding than other municipal amenity areas. However, these landscapes can pose a problem from a design perspective, as the university calendar does not fall in line with the growing season. Special consideration needs to be given to flowering times so that there is visual appeal and interest at the right time. This is particularly important when students return after the summer and when open days occur through the autumn period. To this end, some universities, including Queen Mary's College in East London, trialled swathes of annual flowers. They asked for help from seeding experts Pictorial Meadows to sow the annuals and carry out the maintenance regime. Success would lie within the design and the ability to provide impact for as much of the year as possible.

Installation

Areas of land that had traditionally been mown grass for amenity use were selected for the meadow transformation. After an application of glyphosate, these areas were covered with a layer of green waste compost that provided a sterile base and avoided immediate weed competition. Seed mixes were designed for both vivid colour and longevity of flowering. Another important consideration was the height of the flowers, chosen to provide ever-growing layers through the season. It was almost a 'painting by numbers' approach, where large blocks of colour would provide the impact that was desired. The plants were then cut three times during the first season and in this way the flowering time was managed. If the annual plants chosen had been allowed to set seed in the absence of cutting, they would have stopped flowering; in addition, the cutting provided stronger growth.

Success of the wildflower meadow

The success of a project in an amenity space such as this is judged on public reaction, so design and impact are crucial. Where the displays are well received, further investment will be made along with a commitment to the management of the area, thus providing the knock-on benefits such as biodiversity and carbon sinking. The planting has paved the way for more permanent wildflower displays over time and the benefits these bring.

Above: After glyphosate, green
waste compost was spread
before seeding annual flowers.

Left: The resultant rapid growth
was managed by a cutting
regime that kept the plants
flowering as opposed to setting
seed and senescing.

Left: For campus residents and visitors alike, colourful annuals were a huge improvement on the previous mown lawn monoculture.

Above: Plants were kept flowering to coincide with term times.

Right: After flowering, the annuals set seed and were cut back for winter prior to the cycle starting again in spring.

Meadow on a sloping site

A hard-to-maintain area with pond and steep banks gets a design makeover

LOCATION Rural Sussex
PURPOSE To transform a problematic area into an
outdoor living space.
INSTALLATION METHOD Wildflower turf.
SPECIFIC CHALLENGES A steeply banked site with
immediate results required.
AREA 750 sq m (897 sq yd).

A couple in Sussex wanted to update an area of their
garden that had become neglected. A natural pond had
formed at the base of some steep slopes and this area
of the garden was very difficult to maintain. With such
a tricky site, they decided that any planting needed to
be designed properly and appointed the services of
renowned garden designer Ann-Marie Powell. She created
a stunning 360-degree design, making the best use of the
existing contours while avoiding costly groundworks.

Installation

The contractors, Garden House Design, used a turf-
cutter to peel off the grass and then hand-raked the
site to create a decent tilth. The hard landscaping,
which included stone steps and a decked terrace, was
installed and then the wildflower turf was applied
horizontally, with strips layered like bricks to achieve
a whirlpool effect, circling down to the pond. Because
of the steep slopes, degradable willow pegs were used
to hold the turf in place. The installation took 4–5 men
more than two days as every roll of turf had to be hand-
carried down the hill and into position. Attention to
detail was key in such a well-considered design.

Success of the wildflower meadow

This garden came alive as soon as the turf was laid.
It provided an instant effect and within weeks the
wildflowers were making an impact. It is a wonderful
use of wildflowers, both from a visual perspective
and also as a solution for an area that is a difficult to
maintain. The instantaneous effect meant that the
designer and contractor were able to enter their
stunning work into prestigious garden design and build
award competitions in the same year. The owner has
been delighted with the success of the meadow and
transformation of the garden.

Above: The existing site
was uninspiring and
difficult to maintain.

JAMES SAYS . . .

We repeatedly hear that with most forms of landscaping a professional can supply a high-quality result without too much difficulty, but in the case of sowing wildflowers there can be real problems. Once the meadow is sown the landscaper leaves the area in the hands of the customer, who may struggle with aftercare, unsure which seedlings are weeds, and be unhappy with the time the meadow takes to establish. Wildflower turf eliminates this worry. As soon as it is laid the customer has no responsibilities while it establishes and the designer and landscape contractor will not be called back for remedial work. The client is spending money on a creative project and they want to enjoy it as quickly as possible. Debs Winrow at Garden House Design described using wildflower turf for this project as the bow on the bouquet, the finishing touch that is of huge commercial importance to their business. She said, 'We could walk away from this project safe in the knowledge that the gardener can easily maintain the area and there is little risk of failure of the planting.'

Left: A blanket of wildflowers created a stunning impact and the client was delighted with the minimal maintenance.

Below: The garden just three months after installation, the wildflowers definitely providing the finishing touch.

Right: The mix of soft and hard landscaping in this project was beautifully executed.

From rose garden to meadow

The transformation of an existing rose garden

LOCATION A domestic garden in the south of England.
PURPOSE To provide an inviting usable and low-maintenance garden.
INSTALLATION METHOD Wildflower turf.
SPECIFIC CHALLENGES Reducing soil fertility to aid a successful meadow.
AREA 300 sq m (360 sq yd).

In this stunning project, designer Sean McGeachy was responsible for a complete transformation of an old rose garden that was not performing well in spite of occupying much valuable maintenance time.

The owner decided that he would like to change the area to something he would be more inclined to use. Wildflowers appeared to be the best option for low maintenance, as well as providing an unexpected element once inside the garden, which was entirely enclosed by a high yew hedge. On a visit to Great Dixter in East Sussex, Sean had been inspired by the mix of formal topiary with the fluidity of grasses and wildflowers, and it was decided that a similar juxtaposition would work well here.

Sean researched appropriate methods and decided against seeding on account of the time required for an acceptable result along with the less predictable chance of success. Turf was more likely to provide the best results in the quickest amount of time.

JAMES SAYS . . .

It is the contrast of the formal and informal elements of this garden that make it an inspiring and unexpected design. Topiary or sculpture set among informal wildflowers works really well, for rather than competing with the structure they provide an ever-changing backdrop. Where wildflowers back onto hedges and fences it is important to keep a mown edge between the two. This will help maintenance considerably, particularly for hedge-trimming, while also keeping a more designed feel to the garden.

There is no doubt that the fertilizer used for the roses will have an impact on meadow growth that could last for 3–4 years. When planting wildflowers onto fertile soil you are likely to experience unexpectedly robust growth, and flowers that are particularly tall are more prone to falling over should wind or a heavy downpour take hold in early summer. If this happens you will need to cut back the meadow to 15-20 cm (6-8 in) in June or July, making sure to remove all clippings and therefore reducing the nutrients that would otherwise return to the soil. Cutting in March is also helpful if the grass element of the meadow has grown disproportionately over the winter, particularly if it has been a mild season.

Installation

Preparation work started at the end of the year. The roses and some soil were removed from the garden using heavy machinery which was also put into service to plant the topiary, which was up to 3 m (10 ft) tall. The soil was then levelled and a layer of sand combined to aid drainage. The turf was laid at the beginning of March and irrigated for a month.

Because the area had been quite heavily fertilized for the previous rose garden, Sean kept a close eye on the growth of the grasses. The meadow was very fast-growing and was fully established within the first two months, quickly giving the appearance it had always been there. The meadow was cut with a brush cutter as soon as it started to fade, with the possibility of a second cut the following March if the grass had grown rampantly over the winter period.

Success of the wildflower meadow

The resultant wildflower meadow set against the topiary is now the owner's favourite part of his 2.4 ha (6 acre) garden. Sean believes that wildflowers evoke fond memories for the many visitors who see the area. Overall, it is the sense of well-being that he feels his client most likes, in an area that is incredibly relaxing and inviting throughout the growing season. Further wildflower projects are now planned for other areas of the garden.

Large machinery was required to put the topiary in place but left a muddy mess.

After the soil was level and dried out, the turf was laid at the end of March.

By midsummer the meadow was flourishing. The juxtaposition of
formal and informal elements works well in garden design.

Above: Wildflowers have transformed this garden into a place for relaxation and contemplation.

Above right: Wildflowers provide a stunning backdrop to structural pieces within the garden. A small margin can help define the topiary and allow easy maintenance. This can easily be done retrospectively if needed.

Right: At the end of September the meadow still provides plenty to look at.

Deck with meadow

A small backyard garden combining wildflowers, decking and a hammock

LOCATION Inner-city courtyard garden
PURPOSE To add biodiversity to an otherwise non-biodiverse area.
INSTALLATION METHOD Native perennial wildflower turf.
SPECIFIC CHALLENGES Choosing the right materials for the build to enhance the quality of the wildflowers.
AREA 6 sq m (7 sq yd).

For city-dwellers who work full time and have only a small back-yard space, the idea of creating a green oasis is appealing but rarely achieved. Lack of time for maintenance and a desire for seating space outside leads to many a back yard being concreted over with the addition of patio furniture and a few pots. Garden designer Helen Elks Smith wanted to inspire the city-dweller with this particular show garden to demonstrate how a structured space can still provide a green corridor without requiring a great deal of maintenance.

Installation

The materials chosen are of great importance in this design. The use of natural wood for the walls and decking means there is more heat absorption available compared to that allowed by stone or brick, so this small space is protected from too much transpiration and evaporation. Small beds were defined around the deck and a wooden bench and hammock were added to create a relaxing, immersive environment.

JAMES SAYS . . .

This is an ideal approach for someone who wants to enjoy their garden but does not have the time to maintain it. The meadow becomes an integral part of a small garden and is likely to provide a great deal of interest. Should the owner be inspired to take things further, there would be opportunities for enhancement with plugging and bulbs.

Success of the wildflower meadow

It is amazing to see how layering a design of wood and wildflowers has created a garden that looks more spacious than it really is. While in most cases the hard landscaping would make for an anti-wildlife environment, the wildflowers will encourage pollinators into the garden.

Opposite: Immersive seating is an integral element when using wildflowers in a structured garden design.

Above: Layering with hard and soft landscaping gives the impression of space.

Right: The use of wood aids heat absorption and reduces water loss from an inner-city garden.

Wildflowers for wildlife

There are a number of reasons for establishing a wildflower meadow, but one of the most rewarding is to see the benefit it brings to wildlife. As soon as plants of many different species are established, wildlife species will also arrive in numbers – hence the environmental value placed on this type of habitat.

These case studies show a selection of wildlife-friendly meadows that have been established to encourage wildlife. Their relevance in an educational environment is exciting, offering all sorts of learning opportunities for every age group.

Wildflowers provide a pollen- and nectar-rich food source throughout the spring, summer and autumn when the pollinators are active.

Wildlife meadow

Experimenting with seed and turf

LOCATION A suburban garden in the English midlands
PURPOSE To create a wildlife-friendly back garden.
INSTALLATION METHOD Trialling seed and turf.
SPECIFIC CHALLENGES A DIY project with no experience
of creating wildflower areas.
AREA 50 sq m (60 sq yd).

'Wildlife Kate', also known as Kate MacRae, has
directed her passion for wildlife and role as an
environmental education consultant into a fascinating
project in her garden that has now been seen on
many a wildlife programme on TV. Kate is a keen
photographer and her pictures can be seen on her blog
at www.wildlifekate.co.uk, featuring all of the wildlife
that comes to visit her garden.

In early spring 2014, Kate decided that she would
like to increase the wild habitat in her back garden
to encourage more birds, bees and pollinators for her
to observe and film. A classic long and narrow back
garden, it had mostly been laid to lawn, one side being
particularly shady with a hedge and trees. Kate wanted
to experiment with methods of establishment. She
used two types of wildflower turf, a native perennial
landscape mix for the more open area and a shade-
tolerant mix to lay in the shade of the hedgerow. She
also used a number of wildflower seed mixes in order to
compare the different methods of establishment.

Installation

Prior to laying the turf, Kate scraped off the existing
lawn with a spade and heavy rake and created what
she described as a 'muddy patch'. The seed mixes were
sown into similar conditions. Neither area was treated
with chemicals as Kate is very opposed to using any
within her garden; she feels strongly that the promotion
of biodiverse environments should not require the
killing of all existing plants, with the resulting impact
on wildlife.

Success of the wildflower meadow

The seed trials had varying success but Kate admitted
that she did not give them as much attention as they
probably required. Torrential rain at the start of the
growing season meant that everything grew quickly but
fragile seedlings were damaged, leading to very patchy
growth. She also struggled to tell which seedlings were
wildflowers and which were weeds and as a result, the
latter did take hold of the seeded areas. While Kate felt
her trials weren't scientific enough she thought it likely
that the sown area of wildflowers was established and
maintained in much the same way that most amateur
gardeners would do it.

The turf obviously had more resilience to the heavy
downpours. Within a week there was plenty of growth
and the area started to look very attractive. Kate was
delighted with the flourish of wildflowers, though the
heavy rains in the early part of the growing season
caused the plants to become quite leggy and in places
some either fell or were knocked over by the rain.
In the second year of growth Kate decided to cut half
the meadow area in June and will be looking to see the

impact on flowering in subsequent years. She noticed that campion was dominating throughout May and has decided to cut this specific plant before they shed their seed in order to keep a check on it. Kate sees her garden as an evolving project and will continue to experiment with different techniques.

JAMES SAYS . . .

Kate's knowledge of wildflowers and the wildlife they attract has been exceptional and her regular meadow updates on Twitter (@katemacrae) are followed avidly by about 10,000 followers. I understand a reluctance to use chemicals and where this choice is made, stripping the surface of vegetation is a very good way of controlling weeds. It is hard work if done with a spade, and can be made much easier with the use of a turf cutter. There will be a pile of soil and vegetation to deal with afterwards, but it is certainly possible to make an area clean of weeds and suitably prepared for wildflowers. Using turf will instantly replace the vegetation and benefit the wildlife straightaway. The turf's competitive mat of plants will prevent any weed growth in the scraped soil as the weed seed will not have a chance to germinate and compete.

In Kate's seeded areas, she points out the difficulty in identifying the weeds from the wildflowers at the seedling stage. This is very hard to do and is only slightly easier as the plants develop and mature.

It takes expertise and then patience to remove the weeds, and it is an ongoing job that needs to be done for a few years, since pernicious weeds such as docks (*Rumex obtusifolius*) and nettles (*Urtica dioica*) can quickly spread if they are not removed.

The native versus non-native plant choice is another contentious issue. There has been an in-depth study done by the RHS to look at the effect of natives and non-natives on wildlife, the general findings seem to be that wildlife doesn't mind – it enjoys and can use both. From a non-expert stance it would seem to me that providing there is a ready source of pollen and nectar about, a bee or butterfly will be happy. But it certainly makes sense to consider this at the planning stage and in a rural environment err on the side of natives to remain in keeping with the countryside. In an urban or garden setting there is a choice of either. I think anything in the form of a meadow is better than nothing!

KATE SAYS . . .

Within a week, the turf was starting to establish and after just a month the area had been transformed into a stunning meadow, attracting a wide variety of invertebrates. The different flowering periods mean the turf is always providing a nectar source, as well as shelter, to many different species and I am thrilled with not only how it looks, but also how it has increased the biodiversity within my garden in such a short time. It is the ultimate in low-maintenance wildlife gardening. With regard to the seeds, while it is much cheaper to buy a packet from a garden centre than to bring in turf, it involves a great deal more work and much more uncertainty, particularly for the inexperienced. Interestingly, one of the packets of seeds I bought, which was said to be of British native wildflowers included pictures of monarch butterflies, a species that is native to America not the UK. This immediately made me question the knowledge of those supplying the 'UK native seed' and I started to doubt what I was buying. For this reason I feel more comfortable accepting the costs of turf and know that I am getting guaranteed results with native wildflowers. Wildflowers have changed the feel of my garden completely and it is a definite mood enhancer.

Above: Laying wildflower turf on soil previously cleared of lawn turf.

Below: The wildflower turf areas were more successful than the seeded ones.

Opposite: The turf established quickly and the meadow flourished as the season progressed.

Right: Scabious is a great source of nectar and a magnet for all bees, the plight of bees in the UK is close to Kate's heart.

Below: The successful establishment of so many wildflowers has helped Kate extend her extensive library of wildlife shots.

School meadow

Creating an environment to aid the study of wildlife

LOCATION A suburban school.
PURPOSE To enhance school gardens with wildflowers and encourage wildlife.
INSTALLATION METHOD Native wildflower turf.
SPECIFIC CHALLENGES Getting the timing right so that children could study the life cycle of the plants.
AREA 15 sq m (18 sq yd).

Schools are often set in grounds that have the potential to become outdoor classrooms. With an interested member of staff, even a small space can be converted into an area that is perfect for learning at any stage of the school curriculum. This particular school is in a suburban setting. With a keen groundsman and head teacher, it was possible to embark on creating a learning environment for primary school children that included a pond and wildflower area. A big focus in the early stage curriculum is the study of 'mini beasts' and wildflowers are the perfect magnet for insects and wildlife.

Installation

After the pond had been created and fenced in, the turf was laid around its perimeter. The work took place during the Easter holidays, so that when the children arrived back at school for the summer term they could watch the development of the meadow from small plants to blooming flowers.

JAMES SAYS . . .

We have seen a surge of interest in wildflowers from schools. It is wonderful to see the use of outdoor classrooms involving children with nature from an early age, particularly in urban areas. This was a lovely project to be involved in, seeing the enthusiasm that was nurtured. Creating a meadow in an educational environment, particularly at primary school level, requires immediate results so that the children can get involved from the outset, so the establishment method needs to be reliable and immediate. This school was delighted with the results of their wildflower area and so was I.

Success of the wildflower meadow

Five years later the meadow continues to thrive and is an integral part of the children's learning. The lifecycle of the meadow ties in really well with the school calendar as it is at its best during the summer term, providing plenty of study opportunities. The annual maintenance cut takes place just before the children return to school in September. The rest of the year sees a species-rich carpet teeming with wildlife at the water's edge, allowing the children to have close contact with nature.

Above: Outdoor classrooms framed with wildflowers provide wonderful learning opportunities for all ages. This patch inspired a mini beast art project.

Above right: A pond with a wildflower area is a magnet for wildlife, particularly insects, and provides wide-ranging study opportunities.

Right: Inspiring a love of nature from a young age is essential for the future of our native meadows and wildlife.

Meadow for bees

Creating a nectar-rich habitat for bees and encouraging fruit tree pollination

LOCATION A beekeeper's garden in rural Hampshire
PURPOSE To create a very tasty honey!
INSTALLATION METHOD Native perennial wildflower turf.
SPECIFIC CHALLENGES Adding a bee-friendly setting to aid the bee population.
AREA 18 sq m (21 sq yd).

While many people might imagine that bees would have an idyllic environment in a rural arable landscape, it can be an area where they have little opportunity for nectar collection. Many arable farms, while biodiverse around field margins, are monoculture 'deserts' in the fields themselves. Oil seed rape is a popular arable crop and between May and June this does provide a rich and immediate nectar source encouraging plenty of bee activity, but honey created from the nectar can have a flavour that is less pleasant than the honey from natural planting. Also, the higher glucose content can cause crystalline honey with a gritty texture. This beekeeper wanted to provide a different nectar option for his bee colony during May and June and so decided to plant a small wildflower meadow in front of his hive.

JAMES SAYS . . .

It would have been interesting to interview the bees on this case study to find out which nectar source they prefer! While heather is known to be the best source for honey production, mixed wildflowers with a range of plants blooming throughout the food-gathering season of the solitary and honey bee come a very close second.

Installation

The patch was self-installed after a very small amount of work. The beekeeper was wholly opposed to any chemical intervention and prepared the area by merely digging over a grassy patch and then raking to remove any heavy clumps of soil or grass. The turf was then installed straight onto this patch with a limited amount of watering.

Success of the wildflower meadow

The meadow is in its third year at the time of writing. There is a large coniferous tree and high hedges around the area which do cause a fair amount of shade. Pink and white campions thrive in the shady conditions and provide early-season nectar. Maintenance is sporadic with no particular cutting regime, but despite the random nature of maintenance and the harsher conditions the meadow continues to thrive and the honey produced tastes noticeably better!

Above: This was a small area, requiring just a morning of digging over and raking off.

Right: Wildflower turf was laid in late March, with a lawn turf path laid down the centre of the meadow.

Left: Six weeks later, in mid-May, the pink campion began to flourish.

Below: By mid-June the meadow was a well-established larder for the bees.

Right: Wildflowers provide a rich and abundant nectar source for honey bees.

Wildflower roofs

Over the last decade green roofs have become popular around the world, offering a way to introduce new buildings while providing some environmental compensation. Installing a wildflower meadow on a roof increases biodiversity in an urban area without limiting the space available for building. It can help to camouflage a new build and has practical benefits such as keeping a building cool for its inhabitants as well as providing a quiet, undisturbed and relatively predator-free habitat for the wildlife on the top floor.

The following case studies give an insight into the ways to create a wildflower meadow on a roof. The key things to get right are the level and type of substrate that you use and once this is correct then success is straightforward. Amazing results can be seen with even the most basic DIY projects, such as bike shed roofs and stables, while the award-winning projects encourage new technical developments and enhancements for sustainable buildings. Wildflower roofs provide the perfect way of reinstating what has been lost through development and are sometimes even an improved habitat for wildlife compared to what previously existed at ground level.

Green roofs offer a tremendous opportunity to create a sustainable habitat in the built environment and can mitigate the potentially adverse effects of building developments on wildlife.

Pitched roof

Embedding a new build into a Site of Special Scientific Interest

LOCATION SSSI in the New Forest National Park in southern England.
PURPOSE Creation of a new-build boathouse in an environmentally sensitive setting.
INSTALLATION METHOD Imported growing medium and wildflower roof turf
SPECIFIC CHALLENGES Strict planning regulations.
AREA 200 sq m (239 sq yd).

Avon Tyrrell is a historic manor in the New Forest National Park. Dating back to the 11th century, it now provides the backdrop to a wonderful charity, UK Youth, which provides non-formal learning opportunities. This beautiful site is bound by strict planning regulations and the New Forest National Park Planning Authority provided exact guidelines that the design had to adhere to. HPW, the appointed architectural practice based in the New Forest, have specialized in designing and delivering sustainable buildings for over a decade and the Boathouse was designed to accommodate photo-voltaic panels to collect solar energy and produce electricity.

HPW also proposed a wildflower roof to help immerse the building in the landscape and gain support from all parties. Creating a habitat and food source for indigenous wildlife was particularly important as there were a number of threatened species in the area that would benefit from the wildflowers on the roof.

Installation

The detailing of the green roof for the Boathouse was designed and built using tried and tested principles. Both HPW and Organic Roofs have worked with wildflower turf on a number of different projects and it was the obvious medium to use here as the setting of the Boathouse meant the roof required instant effect and maturity in order to blend with the landscape. Plants appropriate to this location were also essential.

Organic Roofs used Hertalan membrane for waterproofing and developed a specific compression fixing to support the substrate and wildflower turf in layers along the length of a 38-degree pitched roof. This enabled the load-bearing requirements to be reduced and allow for simple finishes to the eaves that would not impact on the 'green' feel to the roof. Lee from Organic Roofs allows for at least 100 mm (4 in) of substrate. 'The quality of substrate and levels used is incredibly important for the health of the green roof. Under-specification of substrate will lead to long-term problems with the sustained growth of wildflowers.'

Success of the wildflower roof

This spectacular project met with many plaudits from all interested parties. The wildflower roof turf was established in a matter of weeks and a strong display of wildflowers seen in the same growing season. The roof will need to be cut with all arisings removed once a year in the autumn.

Right: Bags are used to hold the substrate in place on a steep pitched roof to stop displacement.

Above: The wildflower roof needed to blend immediately into its surroundings and the turf gave an instant greening effect.

Right: The Boathouse generates its own income from the solar panels and will have funded the build within seven years.

Below: This award-winning green roof pioneered techniques that are now adopted for creating pitched wildflower roofs.

Flat Roof

Creating a green flat roof for the Scottish climate

LOCATION Rural area of south-west Scotland
PURPOSE To make a holiday home usable by those with multi-chemical sensitivity.
INSTALLATION METHOD Wildflower roof turf.
SPECIFIC CHALLENGES The roof needed to be suitable for long periods of cold weather.
AREA 60 sq m (72 sq yd).

Durhamhill is a listed farmhouse nestled among hills, lochs and woodland on the south-west coast of Scotland. Juliet and Alan decided to turn their disused farm buildings into a holiday home and wanted to create an eco-friendly conversion incorporating an open-plan extension from which to look out onto the striking landscape. The fields and meadow banks that surround the house are completely organic; Juliet has multi-chemical sensitivity and over the years she and Alan have made sure that no pesticides or chemicals have been used on the land that now is home to her pet llamas. Her choice of building materials and furnishings were of great importance, as was the desire for the extension to have minimal impact on the view.

The architect had originally suggested using sedum on the flat roof extension. It has been the plant of choice for green roofs for a number of years, though most sedum roofs are composed of few species, limiting their benefit to biodiversity. It is also debatable how much of a natural look is created, but sedum can survive on very little fertility and water and this has made it popular. Recently, however, the environmental shortcomings of sedum have created a lot of interest in

JAMES SAYS . . .

Roofs are independent of local soil conditions and have a micro-climate all of their own. The growing medium and moisture can be manipulated to influence the look of the roof. I favour a high organic content in the substrate as this will help to retain moisture for the plants; making the substrate too free-draining will quickly dry out the roof meadow and more watering will be required to avoid the plants going into drought mode and turning brown. Using a high organic content (80–100 per cent) will help the substrate layer act like a sponge, holding water for the plants to use if weather conditions dry up. Organic growing mediums still allow excess water to drain away quickly.

Wildflowers are remarkably hardy and if anything, a layer of snow will help to protect them against the ravages of strong, cold winds. Either way, cold conditions and short day length cause the plants to become dormant. As daylight increases and the warmer spring weather takes hold, this dormancy breaks and rapid growth is apparent. Extreme examples of the influence of seasonal variation can be seen in Scandinavia. Traditional Norwegian green roofs remain covered in snow and only see minimal light for many months through the winter. These roofs emerge in the spring with vibrant growth as plants rush through their growth stages to make the most of the warmth and 24-hour light through the summer.

species-rich wildflower meadows as a better choice for use on green roofs.

Juliet wanted the view from the meadow to the building and beyond to be seamless and she was keen to encourage more biodiversity. After researching the options she discovered wildflower turf and decided it would be perfect for their site and needs. The couple had to apply for planning permission and the use of a biodiversity-enhancing roof material definitely helped their case. In addition Juliet was pleased to discover that wildflower turf was a cheaper option to the sedum system they had originally considered.

Installation

Local craftsmen were used for the building works and the turf was installed in just one day during October. The winter following installation was a particularly harsh one and the wildflower roof lay under snow for several weeks in March, followed by endless rain. Juliet and Alan were a little worried about how the wildflower roof would cope but during April there were early signs of growth and the first flowers could be seen in May. Their initial fears about the turf establishing were overtaken by astonishment at how quickly the wildflowers were flourishing. Juliet describes an ever-changing sea of colour that remained until strimming took place in October.

Success of the wildflower roof

With wildflower roofs, consideration should be given to irrigation during long dry periods of the summer but given their location Juliet and Alan decided against fixed irrigation. Easy access to the roof means they can use a sprinkler if and when the need arises. Juliet described the maintenance required as 'really minimal' and 'well worth it' for the constant admiration it receives from all of their visitors.

Juliet and Alan have definitely noticed an increase in wildlife, in particular bees and moths. An enthusiast who came to stay saw a very rare species of moth that had been attracted to the flowers on the roof. Juliet says, 'The outstanding feature of the wildflower roof is how well it has blended with the surrounding landscape and within just a year, it looks as if it has been there forever.'

Installation of the growing medium. Bagged substrate around the perimeter helps to maintain an even depth of substrate while retaining the loose material.

Left: Once the growing medium is in place the wildflower turf is quickly laid over it.

Right: The height of the wildflowers makes them very visible from the ground, even on a flat roof.

Below: Og the cat now has a comfortable vantage point!

Below right: The outstanding feature of the wildflower roof is how well it has blended with the surrounding landscape.

Visitor Centre Roof

Creative and inspiring green roof design

LOCATION A theme park in southern England.
PURPOSE To install a large-scale green roof project on a highly populated visitor centre.
INSTALLATION METHOD Wildflower roof turf
SPECIFIC CHALLENGES Maintaining a large green roof so that it looks in good order year round.
AREA 920 sq m (1100 sq yd).

Paultons Family Theme Park, located in the south of England, hoped to achieve international status with its pioneering sustainable design and low-cost operation of the park's Peppa Pig World attraction. One of the main features of the visitor building was a curved wildflower roof, which was crucial in securing planning in an environmentally sensitive location. The park is open all year round, so the roof needed to look appealing throughout the seasons without having a long browning-off period while the flowers senesce. The biggest challenge was therefore going to be the maintenance.

> **JAMES SAYS . . .**
>
> A wildflower meadow is incredibly drought-resistant and if planted on free-draining soil is unlikely ever to need watering beyond installation. Wildflowers generally have extensive root systems that bury themselves very deep into the ground, often 1–2 m (3½–6½ ft) down, which allows them to stay alive even in times of drought. On a roof, they are not able to form these deep root systems so on a large-scale installation such as this a drip-feed irrigation system is a good idea. However, watering is only required after 10 days without precipitation. Without a good source of moisture the wildflowers will simply flower very quickly in order to produce seed and be viable again for next year so, while the irrigation is not essential, it will keep the roof flowering for longer and looking greener which is perhaps more desirable in such a highly populated attraction park.

Installation

The installation took place during a very dry period. The substrate was laid onto the roof in onion bags in order for the curvature of the roof to be retained without the substrate slipping to the base of the roof. The architects had specified a 110 mm (4½ in) layer of substrate and screed was then put on top to level off any minor undulations. An advanced computerized irrigation system was also installed at the same time to drip-irrigate during the growing season in coming years. However, when first installed the turf required watering from the top down to help the establishment of the root system. Roots will grow quickly to find a water source, so once the turf was laid sprinklers were used for the first month.

Success of the wildflower roof

In the first year of opening the attraction received more than 1 million visitors. The turf had performed well and provided plenty of colour and variation through the first summer. During the winter it was noticeable that parts of the roof were dying off. It was discovered that the irrigation had not been switched off until the end of September and the roof was suffering from over-watering. The following growing season saw a reduction in the irrigation, watering only in particularly dry periods, and the bare patches soon came back to full health. A 'mansafe' clip-on harness system was added to the roof to enable safe maintenance. The roof still receives only one maintenance cut a year, just after the meadow has browned off. It remains a green roof project held in very high regard for the sheer scale and health of the wildflowers.

Top right: Substrate in non-degradable onion sacks helps to retain the shape of the roof.

Centre right: The sacks are then screed to level off the surface before laying the turf.

Right: A 'mansafe' system is put in place on large-scale roofs for safety during maintenance.

The resulting
meadow offers
a unique visual
scene as well as an
amazing habitat for
wildlife.

The curved
nature of the
roof is a stand-
out feature of
this award-
winning design.

Over-watering can
cause a wildflower roof
to die off.

Stable Roof

An alternative stable roof that keeps the visual appeal of a green roof year round.

LOCATION Wildflower Turf headquarters, Hampshire
PURPOSE A wildflower roof to insulate and camouflage a new-build stable.
INSTALLATION METHOD Wildflower roof turf.
SPECIFIC CHALLENGES A research and development project to pave the way for the development of a specific roof turf.
AREA 90 sq m (108 sq yd).

This was a pilot project using a bespoke wildflower turf on a roofing system. The chosen building was a new stable. As well as acting as a test project the green roof was intended to camouflage the building and provide insulation to the horses below. The roof structure included additional trusses to take the extra weight and a bespoke liner gave a tidy finish to the corners and edges while guaranteeing no leaks.

Installation

Non-degradable sacks of substrate were used around the perimeter edge of the roof and along the ridge in order to keep the depth of the soil even. The voids were then filled with loose substrate to a depth of 100 mm (4 in). Drip irrigation was also added. Wildflower turf was laid on top.

Success of the wildflower roof

The roof is now in its tenth year and continues to look good as a biodiverse and beautiful topping to a stable.

With hindsight, we should have increased the substrate depth as we did not account for settlement and this trial taught us to allow 10 per cent extra to overcome this. Wildflowers transpire a great deal more than sedum, the alternative green roof option at the time. Limiting plant root depth reduces available water and can shorten flowering time.

For trial purposes, this roof has been allowed to dry out over a number of summers. After a dry spell of more than a few weeks, the roof browns off quickly. This is especially noticeable each side of the summer solstice when long, sunny days will take their toll on the plants. South-facing roof slopes will suffer most and windy days quickly draw out moisture from the plants. It has been interesting to note that in spite of this harsh treatment the number of plant species is as strong as ever. Because the plants were allowed to establish with early irrigation, this tough environment has delivered healthy plant diversity over the life of the roof.

We continue to use this roof as a testing ground with a recent trial of spring bulbs. We chose low-growing varieties that bloom from February to May, such as crocus, *Iris reticulata*, fritillaria, miniature narcissi and dwarf tulips. The bulbs were planted by hand using a bulb-planting tool, going into the roof at a diagonal angle to make sure the underlying waterproofing was not damaged. The results were fantastic and gave the extra colour and impact that we wanted early in the year.

JAMES SAYS . . .

This was very much a last-minute project and the stable was not given a detailed design. I recommend the use of a structural engineer and waterproofing specialist for all roofs, though I have seen many very successful DIY projects on garden offices and sheds using shop-bought pond liners and soil from the footings, capped with wildflowers. They work and are relatively inexpensive but some of the detailed finishes around gutters and upstands can be a little untidy.

This stable roof has given us a great deal of confidence in the ability of wildflowers to thrive on a rooftop and provide an alternative and visually impressive finish.

Above right: A simple timber upstand helps to retain the substrate.

Right: Bags of substrate around the margins and down the ridge allow an infill of loose substrate.

Below: An even depth and smooth finish was created, ready for the turf.

Bottom: Drip irrigation above the substrate and below the turf was installed.

Right: Spring-flowering bulbs were planted for early-season colour.

Above: As the season progresses, wildflowers emerge and overtake the bulbs.

Left: The end result makes a naturalistic environment for its inhabitants.

Challenging sites

While there are many sites that are suitable for a wildflower meadow, problems can arise before and after establishment. The robust and enduring nature of wildflowers will help with long-term success, but giving thought to the site and its preparation will improve the prospects of the meadow and reduce the time taken. Embarking on a project involving living plants can be similar to actors never wanting to work with children or animals; they are unpredictable, so you can never be quite sure of what you are going to get!

The following case studies show examples of how to overcome problem areas such as coastal sites, roadside verges, steep banks and shady areas. There is also a fascinating story of how meadows have completely transformed areas of wasteland in Sheffield. If there are difficulties with your site, the key thing is not to be deterred; time and work will normally provide success in the long term. Perennial wildflowers are hardy, enjoying harsh conditions, and they can be a solution where other plants haven't been able to thrive.

Challenging sites will often hold opportunities for wildflowers. Once established, the long term nature and low maintenance requirements of wildflowers often work where alternative options do not.

CASE STUDY 16

Meadow by the sea

A wildflower meadow for a modern home by the sea

LOCATION A windy coastal garden in Suffolk.

PURPOSE To create a low-maintenance garden for a holiday home that will allow the property to blend into its surroundings.

INSTALLATION METHOD Bespoke wildflower turf.

SPECIFIC CHALLENGES Creating a bespoke turf with species suitable for windswept salt marshes.

AREA 3000 sq m (3588 sq yd).

This superb property on the Suffolk coast was bought specifically with the view over an expansive estuary in mind. Completely rebuilt by Soup Architects, the house has since won design awards. Landscape designer Christine Hatt was appointed by the owners to create a suitable landscape to surround the property and blend it into the surrounding environment. Previously, there had been an established mature garden with flowerbeds and plenty of trees that somewhat hindered the views across the seascape.

There were a number of factors that led to the decision to create a wildflower meadow as the key theme of the garden. Low maintenance was a must-have with such a large area and the soil was very sandy and low in nutrients, so it would have required a great deal of input both with regard to man hours and soil improvers to make it into a productive garden.

With inspiration from the wildflower landscape at Hackney Marshes and the writing of Christopher Lloyd, the creation of a wildflower meadow became very appealing, with the week-to-week changes reflecting the influence of the seasons on the surrounding landscape. Having taken on a lengthy rebuild of the house, the owner was also keen to finish the landscaping as quickly as possible so that she could start enjoying this incredible space. To naturalize the area would have taken far too long and seeding it was risky in such a challenging setting. By using a pre-grown wildflower turf, both owner and designer felt the results could be guaranteed on an exceptionally dry and windy site.

Wildflower Turf were asked to grow a bespoke mix that was designed to thrive in these harsh conditions of salt spray, wind and a low-nutrient, drought-prone soil. The main change from the standard native wildflower mix was to increase the species of grass. While this wouldn't normally be recommended, the harshness of the site and its low-nutrient status meant that the grass wouldn't dominate. Where nutrients and moisture are more available, too much grass results in a lack of wildflower species and therefore colour. In addition to the yellow oatgrass (*Trisetum flavescens*), sweet vernal grass (*Anthoxanthum odoratum*) and quaking grass (*Briza maxima*), we added dame's violet (*Hesperis matronalis*), kidney vetch (*Anthyllis vulneraria*), pepper saxifrage (*Silaum silaus*), sainfoin (*Onobrychis viciifolia*), spiny restharrow (*Ononis spinosa*), wild marjoram (*Origanum vulgare*) and wild mignonette (*Reseda lutea*) for additional colour and fortitude.

Installation

The turf was laid in October in a very cold and wet period of weather. The contractors were especially

JAMES SAYS . . .

This garden gave us a great opportunity to show what wildflowers could bring to a very challenging site. Interestingly the first year showed significant growth – by the sound of it a bit too much! But this is sure to calm down in subsequent years. Wildflowers do well where they are treated a little harshly, and while this site will deliver that in spades, the first year threw up an anomaly because of plentiful moisture and reasonable fertility provided in the growing medium of the turf. This is no bad thing as it ensures good and deep root development for future years when the going is bound to get tougher.

The early cut is none the less a very good idea. In this difficult site, keeping the height down will help to keep the meadow looking good as excessive growth at a windy site is likely to end with a tangled jungle of plant material. The need for the early cut may reduce as the fertility of the area settles down after the ground work and turf installation. The free draining sandy site will lose any excess nutrition through leaching and the autumn removal of material will lower nutrients further. As time goes on Christine will be able to assess the height of the meadow and manage the cutting regime accordingly.

sceptical about how the meadow would look when cut down in subsequent years and therefore prepared the ground as if lawn turf were being laid, levelling out any lumps and bumps. The turf had an instant impact on the site; what had been soil and rubble for almost two years became a wonderful expanse of green and any initial worries were immediately lifted.

Success of the wildflower meadow

In the first spring the growth of the wildflowers was extreme, probably due to the very wet start that the turf had over the winter months. Christine described the growth as almost too successful, having not anticipated that the meadow would be so tall there would soon be a need to cut meandering paths in order to pass from one place to another. Now the meadow is cut in late May or early June to keep the growth in check and the view across the estuary uninterrupted.

Right: A large-scale project, the intention was to completely immerse the new home in wildflowers.

Far right: The view to the salt marshes: the wildflowers smoothed the transition from garden to surrounding landscape.

Below: Additional species in the bespoke turf were specifically chosen for their tolerance of salt and wind.

Left: After a dry summer the wildflowers showed drought tolerance on this this sandy soil.

Bottom: The area close to the kitchen has been cut back to give a species-rich lawn and a transitional view to the meadow beyond.

Roadside verge

A domestic project enhances a roadside verge

LOCATION A suburban roadside verge.
PURPOSE A residential project to beautify a boundary wall and verge.
INSTALLATION METHOD Wildflower turf using natives and non-natives for extra colour and longevity.
SPECIFIC CHALLENGES Establishing wildflowers on an uncultivated piece of land.
AREA 20 sq m (24 sq yd).

Ken and Norma's house lies on a busy road in a village. With the arrival of grandchildren to their family the proximity of the road to the house became a worry, since the traditional shrubbery and mixed hedge that bordered their garden offered little protection from speeding cars. For this reason, they decided to add secure gates and replace the hedge with a brick wall. Having visited the Hampton Court Garden Show to gain some ideas for their new front garden, they had been inspired by a display of wildflower turf and decided to create a wildflower area to soften the look of the wall and cut down on maintenance of the area.

The couple share a passion for wildlife and had considered wildflowers in the garden a number of years earlier, knowing that even a small patch would be beneficial to bees and butterflies. They had experimented with sowing wildflower seeds but had had little joy, gaining poppies but not much else, so they felt wildflower turf was definitely the best method of establishment for their particular project. It would avoid bare soil on the roadside that would probably end up as a muddy strip, particularly at the time of year in question – late autumn. The turf would give them the chance to green up the area as quickly as possible and they chose a native and non-native mix that would prolong the flowering season as well as adding in some brighter colour with poppies, dianthus, calendula and blue flax. After the building works there was not a great deal of soil, so they sourced a low-fertility subsoil to add on top of the area in front of the wall.

Installation

As it was a small area Ken and Norma took on the installation work themselves, laying the turf in no time at all. There was no need to water it in the autumn. They were surprised at how quickly the turf took, with signs of 'greening up' within weeks of laying it despite the approach of winter. They decided to put in wooden poles to act as bollards to prevent traffic encroaching on the turf while it was establishing.

Success of the wildflower meadow

When we spoke to Norma the wildflower turf had been laid just six months before. The couple had not been expecting to see many flowers soon after laying the turf, but the results were instant. They are delighted with how the wildflowers have softened the wall and many passersby have made positive comments. While the wall blocks their view of any increase in wildlife activity, they have enjoyed the changing palette of colour, with no two weeks looking the same during the summer period.

As the turf has some non-native varieties with later

flowering times, Ken and Norma have decided to cut only when necessary later on in the year. The verge no longer needs cutting every couple of weeks and this has been a positive change for them. Asked if they would use the same method for creating a wildflower patch again, Norma answered that they have already started planning a new area for their back garden!

JAMES SAYS . . .

This is a great little project for urban and country homes alike. Wildflowers can be used to great effect to distract attention from harsher lines such as brick walls or even to disguise the legs of a trampoline in a small back garden. Roadside verges outside houses are often neglected and not only will this soon prettify the area, there is a definite decrease in the maintenance required in comparison to a grass verge or green hedge. A strip of wildflowers just 1 m (3¼ ft) in width can provide essential wildlife corridors along main roads and other harsh landscapes. However, where small areas of wildflowers are concerned, maintaining interest and enthusiasm with quick and reliable results is a must.

Top right: Wildflowers are a low-maintenance and highly beneficial solution to difficult-to-manage roadside verges.

Right: Adding non-natives within the turf helps to add colour and interest – perfect for this type of use.

Wildflower bank

Finding a solution for steep banks

LOCATION A historic site, open to the public.

PURPOSE To provide a low-maintenance solution for an area that had become neglected.

INSTALLATION METHOD Wildflower turf.

SPECIFIC CHALLENGES Steep banks make this site very difficult to manage.

AREA 900 sq m (1077 sq yd).

Chichester North Walls is a prestigious site owned by English Heritage. Chichester District Council, which is responsible for the maintenance of the area, had received money from the Heritage Lottery Fund for archaeological investigations as well as the development of a City Walls Trail. The banks of the Walls behind the County Hall had become an eyesore, turning into a mass of nettles and thistles in recent years. Mowing the banks had proved to be a health and safety hazard as the steepness meant that workers needed to use safety harnesses. The steep angle also meant that creating a wildflower area from seed or through naturalizing would be very difficult. Therefore wildflower turf seemed to be the obvious choice to alleviate the operational problems as well as to immediately improve the visual aspects of the site.

Installation

English Heritage have imposed restrictions on ground works and the nature of the site, another aspect that made wildflower turf the right choice as the site would not require a high level of maintenance. The site was cleared with glyphosate and taken back to bare soil. A light tilth was created and then the turf was laid over the top in October. Wooden pegs were used to hold it in place. A total of 900 sq m (1077 sq yd) of landscape turf was used, specifically chosen for its 34 native perennial species, suitable for particularly dry areas with consecutive flowering from April to September. It was given a light watering-in but no further irrigation was needed.

Success of the wildflower meadow

By the following May the meadow bank area was in full bloom. Justin Jones, the Green Spaces Officer responsible for the project, has reported that the benefits have been two-fold: the visual impact of the banked area is improved, while the greatly reduced maintenance requirements have lessened costs. A side flail cutter and a man with a leaf blower is all that is required once a year compared to a team of workers, strimming and raking on a regular basis. There have been many positive comments and much public interest has been expressed in this project.

Steep banks are extremely problematic to maintain as access is often difficult for machinery. Especially in the case of banks adjacent to busy roads, any work carried out can be hazardous. Wildflower turf provides the perfect solution as it requires little maintenance – just one cut per year. The dense and deep root penetration of the wildflowers aids soil retention on the bank. Wildflowers also provide the added benefits of colour, food source for wildlife and habitat creation.

Top: Turfing the banks with wildflowers provided the ideal solution to maintaining this challenging site.

Top centre: The turf not only stabilizes the bank but provides a dense root mat that is difficult for weeds to penetrate.

Right: The resultant wildflowers have completely transformed this historic site.

Shady meadow

Creating an area of interest in a highly shaded part of the garden

LOCATION A woodland area in a domestic garden.
PURPOSE To create a wildflower area in a location that is hard to cultivate.
INSTALLATION METHOD Wildflower earth.
SPECIFIC CHALLENGES A dense tree canopy affecting anything that grows underneath.
AREA 720 sq m (861 sq yd).

This installation was for a new house surrounded by a sizeable garden in a rural location. A number of trees under Tree Protection Orders meant that there was a wooded part of the garden that was difficult to cultivate because of the heavy shade cast by the trees. It had housed chickens so the soil was reasonably fertile and the area had become a weed patch that included a lot of self-sown sycamore and elder shrubs.

The trees underwent a robust crown-lifting programme to increase the light to the ground and reduce the leaf litter to some extent. The wooded area is in the rough shape of an oval and the meadow followed this line to the edge of the tree canopy. Here it met the formal lawn that makes up the bulk of the rest of the garden. This was cleared a year in advance. It then had three doses of glyphosate in the autumn, the spring and then late summer.

Installation

The meadow was installed using the wildflower earth system. Installation was in early September and germination was quick following a few days of rain. Since installation the meadow has been enhanced with naturalizing spring bulbs to give early colour and interest and tall summer bulbs such as allium.

Success of the wildflower meadow

The meadow has taken a couple of years to flourish. The high weed seed content of the soil before the meadow was created has meant there are still some undesirable plants such as cow parsley and nettles and attempts are made to take these out each year. At the very least, seedheads are removed to prevent them setting seed. There is also some spot spraying in the spring. A selection of shade-tolerant bulbs including bluebells and fritillaries was chosen to cope with the conditions. For a little more summer colour a risk was taken with alliums, which have performed fantastically well.

Mown paths have opened up the middle of the wooded area allowing easy access to the other side of the meadow. By looking after the lawn around the meadow with regular mowing and occasional fertilizer applications this formal lawn remains in good health and any possible spread of wildflowers has been controlled.

Top right: The wildflowers have done well with the available light, but leaf litter has been removed each year.

RIght centre: Spring and summer bulbs, such as these alliums, were added to improve colour.

Right: Seven years later the meadow is still thriving despite the shade. This is helped by the crown lift at the start of the project. Heavy shade found in woodlands will not be conducive to wildflower meadow survival and should be avoided.

JAMES SAYS . . .

This was one of the early installations of wildflower earth and despite some difficult conditions the results have been good, even if there is some ongoing work to keep the meadow in shape. The fact that this area is in shade for most of the year has had an effect on the plants that are thriving. In the more heavily shaded areas there is less colour and diversity, but there is enough variety to keep the meadow look and these areas blend well enough for only the practised eye to spot. The meadow has proved to be a great wildlife haven with plenty of bee and butterfly activity. One of the trees has been allowed to keep a dense ivy cladding and this provides a home for a flourishing bat population that no doubt benefits from the insect food source in the area of the meadow.

CASE STUDY 20

High-profile, public site

Creating impact with wildflowers in a high-profile site

LOCATION Athletes' Village, the Olympic Park in the East End of London.

PURPOSE To create a varied landscape with floral interest and benefit to wildlife for this new development.

INSTALLATION METHOD A variety of bespoke-grown wildflower turf mixes.

SPECIFIC CHALLENGES Creating a number of different meadows for species diversity on a very tight timescale for a benchmark-setting project.

AREA 10,000 sq m (11960 sq yd).

This project took place over a number of different sites in the Athletes' Village of the 2012 Olympic Games, now known as Victory Park in the East Village, Stratford, London. The project covered a range of wildflower mixes, from marshy grassland and woodland meadows to species-rich lawns and open pasture. Because of construction delays and the non-negotiable date for the opening of the Olympics, the contractors needed to be sure that all wildflower options would work reliably. Much of the soil was manipulated to account for the high levels of pollution that existed on the site. The remit was to create site-specific conditions for the range of intended habitats, providing an inert and weed-free starting point. In the same way the wildflower mixes were chosen by ecologists specifically to develop these habitats. This was to be a landscaping project that would set standards for urban biodiversity and the use of species certified as native to the UK. At the same time, the site had to provide visual impact for

JAMES SAYS . . .

We were delighted and proud to be involved with this Olympic project and it was particularly interesting to work with the ecologist, architect, site manager and contractor to deliver a solution that performed so well for all. Established plants being delivered to the site as wildflower mats took the pressure off all the stakeholders, producing instant results. The landscape architect wanted to be sure that the mix would have the visual impact required and the contractor wanted a solution that worked within the tight timescales; the ecologist wanted to deliver biodiversity that would be long-lasting and beneficial and the site manager, like everyone, wanted an easy life! In this situation, a pre-grown mat of wildflowers gave the assurance that all parties needed, providing the finished article as opposed to a work in progress.

the visiting athletes and an ongoing legacy to meet the ideals of the 2012 Olympic Delivery Authority.

Wildflower Turf Ltd were commissioned to produce a series of bespoke turf products that would guarantee immediate results. The seed mix was developed in conjunction with the ecologists Biodiversity by Design and the landscape architects Applied Landscape Design.

Installation

The various types of wildflower turf were ready for installation in autumn 2011. A species-rich turf

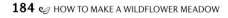

specifically designed for this site was used as an alternative to a standard grass lawn. The aim was to improve the biodiversity rating of the lawn area by using a hard-wearing grass mix, but with the inclusion of wildflowers that could withstand wear and mowing. This idea was developed by the ecologists to help the site meet strict audits for environmental standards and the product has now been accepted as a good way to increase the biodiversity of many new-build sites. In other areas, a specific shade-tolerant mix was developed to go under newly planted trees, some up to 12 m (40 ft) tall. Marshy areas around a series of ponds used turf grown with species such as water mint (*Mentha aquatica*), soft rush (*Juncus effusus*) and hemp agrimony (*Eupatorium cannabinum*), while the open meadow areas were laid with turf that included native species found in the Thames basin. The combination of forward-thinking planners, designers and ecologists transformed the area from industrial wasteland to a site fit to host the biggest event the country has ever held.

Success of the wildflower meadow

In all areas, the wildflower turf delivered immediate results and helped to reduce the pressure on all those responsible for having the site ready for July 2012. Huge attention to detail from those overseeing the site paid dividends and the results were spectacular. Since 2012 a simple but thorough maintenance programme has meant that the objective to provide a legacy of long-term biodiversity and colour has been easily achieved.

The species-rich lawn has been a revelation for a number of reasons. The legumes in the sward have fixed enough nitrogen to keep the area healthy and green with the unexpected result of a negligible amount of artificial fertilizer being applied compared to adjacent areas of standard lawn. In 2013 a neighbouring area of hundreds of square meters of conventional lawn was savaged by an invasion of leatherjackets, which killed off a swathe of grass 2 m (6½ ft) from the edge of a path,

yet just the other side of the path the species-rich lawn did not suffer at all. The high number and variety of species in this area, as well as the density and health of the plants, prevented the ingress of leatherjackets and entirely avoided any damage.

Installing the wildflower turf mats on one of the sites at the Athletes' Village.

Seen here flowering the following spring, the site has been easy to manage and has delivered the biodiverse environment demanded by sustainable initiatives such as the Code for Sustainable Homes.

Opposite top: The species-rich lawn was the first of its kind, developed specifically for this site. The principle of biodiverse lawns is now being used around the country.

Opposite below: Shade-tolerant mats of wildflowers were installed in anticipation of the future growth of the large number of trees that were planted to help naturalize the parkland surrounding the Athletes' Village.

Below: Bespoke marshy grassland turf was grown to complement various ponds around the site.

Below: One of the far-sighted ideas to emerge from this development was the use of detailed, informative interpretation boards that helped to engage the public with the aims of the park and gardens.

Bottom: In contrast to the turfed areas, some of the seeded sections required further explanation!

Below right: Six years after installation, East Village offers an on-going legacy to the time and effort that went into the landscape development for the 2012 Olympic Games.

Community projects

Where urban green spaces are used by the public there can be a lot of resistance to a wildflower meadow with its 'no mow' approach as some people perceive it as the local council cutting costs and leaving things scruffy. This sentiment is set to change as more is being done to raise awareness of the plight of the pollinators and the benefits of wilder green spaces, helping the public understand the genuine reasons for embracing the environment. There is also a wonderful surge in volunteer groups and 'guerrilla gardeners' who are taking on guardianship of areas to create spaces that are beneficial to all. It is indeed an exciting time for green infrastructure.

One way to help a planned meadow be accepted in a public space is to engage with the community that lives nearby. Getting people involved from the planning through to the installation can be enjoyable for all concerned and gives a sense of ownership. If this isn't possible, the use of interpretation boards to explain the reasons for wildflowers and species-rich planting works well. Once the local residents take an interest, it is important to get good results in a short time and successful establishment becomes essential.

The following case studies illustrate how wildflowers can be a mood-changer, both personally and within a community. Contact with nature provides an all-important sense of well-being and wonderful learning opportunities and a meadow can even change perceptions of run-down areas.

Waterfront meadow

Making a riverside micro-meadow

LOCATION River bank, Marlborough, Wiltshire.
PURPOSE To create a micro-meadow on a waterfront site.
INSTALLATION METHOD Wildflower turf
SPECIFIC CHALLENGES Encouraging community involvement to encourage a sense of ownership.
AREA 10 sq m (12 sq yd).

Marlborough is lucky to have a group of residents who are looking after the waterfront, close to the centre of town. In 2013 a new flood wall was constructed, the river was narrowed and land on the river margins was left bare and in need of attention. Val Compton, a resident of the area, had chosen the 'guerrilla gardening' route to maintaining an attractive waterfront in the past, but with this new area to improve she decided to formalize her approach. So the local residents and businesses formed the Marlborough Waterfront Association, keen to create a wild area that would benefit wildlife but also look pretty for the many visitors to the area.

To make best use of the nutrient-rich soil the area was initially sown with bee-friendly annual seeds which gave a great result but was not necessarily in keeping with the wild concept the Association desired. The following year although they had scattered all of the seed heads from the existing plants, there was an invasion of rose bay willow herb, thistle, nettle and dock and very little else got a look in. The vegetation looked somewhat neglected and grew to over 2 m (6½ ft) tall. A different solution was required and the Association sought the permission of Wiltshire Council to dig out 10 sq m (12 sq yd), clearing all roots over winter and hoeing the weed seedlings that emerged in spring prior to establishing a meadow.

Installation

After a great deal of research the Association decided that the best way forward was to use wildflower turf. Val organized a series of fundraising events to pay for the turf including the repotting and selling of plants that had been used for council displays and signing up to community funding projects. With the area thoroughly prepared by the residents, the turf was laid in mid-April. It was very quick to install and residents were surprised at how manageable the turf was.

Success of the wildflower meadow

While residents were sceptical about the wildflowers, they were delighted to see flowers on the turf within two days of it being laid. The first three months of planting saw massed flowers, which had a huge impact on the way people felt about the area and also on the wildlife that was seen. Water voles are now nesting close to the wildflowers and it is hoped that the green cover will provide habitat for a nesting pair over the winter. Maintenance is carried out with hand shears to provide minimal disruption to the wildlife species that have made this area their home.

The Association is now looking at a much wider community project as so many people have expressed a desire to try a small patch of wildflowers in their gardens. By ordering together they hope to share delivery charges to encourage more people to participate and hopefully bring micro meadows to more parts of Marlborough. The volunteer group are also in talks with a new-build developer about dedicating land to wildflowers as well as proposing more wildflower areas to the council.

JAMES SAYS . . .

The Marlborough Waterfront Association study tells a great micro-meadow story. Not only does it include wildlife and visual improvement, it also brings in the idea of community participation. The more people that are involved with the installation of a meadow the better, as everyone is kept informed of the point of a wildflower area and a sense of ownership develops. It is great to hear how just a small patch of wildflowers improved the location and enthused the residents.

Left: The winter of discontent; a mass of weeds leads to the Marlborough Waterfront Association deciding to create a micro-meadow.

Below left: Early May, two weeks after the turf was laid.

Below right: Midsummer and the meadow is established with plenty of species diversity.

Right: The waterside location has proved to be an excellent spot, keeping the meadow green throughout August.

Below: With its close proximity to the wildflowers, the local café has helped to develop an avid meadow following and other wildflower projects are springing up throughout Marlborough.

Eye-catching park and roundabout

Beautifying a roundabout and park with red annual wildflowers

LOCATION Memorial Park, Basingstoke and Deane Borough Council.
PURPOSE To create eye-catching displays in high-visibility areas.
INSTALLATION METHOD Wildflower earth.
SPECIFIC CHALLENGES Planting an entirely red-flowered wildflower mix with annuals.
AREA 540 sq m (646 sq yd)

Basingstoke and Deane Borough Council had previously seeded areas of wildflower on a roundabout close to Basingstoke centre and in the main recreational park within the town centre with only limited success, mainly because of the growth of weeds. The council had pledged an increase in biodiversity among their maintained open spaces, and it was important that the areas would have visual impact and that the wildflower meadows would be created within one season.

Installation

The site was sprayed using a glyphosate herbicide. Because of the previous problems with weeds a second spray was recommended to make sure the areas were as clean as possible from weed seeds but this did not take place for lack of time. Weed regrowth was low in the park but the roundabout had a lot of existing weeds from previous seeded attempts and the seed burden was feared to be quite high. The wildflower earth was applied to both areas with a specialist mix of red annuals including four different types of poppies. The

JAMES SAYS . . .

This type of application is perfect for a site without an existing weed seed burden as it is easy to spread and install. While spraying with herbicide is essential, no rotovation of underlying soil is required. A limiting factor is the time of year; installation can only take place in the spring and autumn and any heavy rains will risk washing away the earth. A small amount of spot-weeding will be required for stubborn weeds. Sow thistle was identified in the park in the first-year display and ideally it would have been removed to avoid a greater weed seed burden. The poppy display was repeated for a second year and there was a greater invasion of sow thistle compared to the previous year.

There is an old adage that goes 'one year seeding, seven years weeding' and certainly if you do not rogue out weeds you are likely to be invaded by a much greater number of plants in subsequent years – it is a weed's way of ensuring survival. It is very important to be on the ball when dealing with weeds as prevention is much easier than cure. Any wildflower meadow can be prone to weed invasion but pictorial meadows that require an annual sowing will be even more likely to suffer and action should be taken as early as possible in the life of the meadow.

area was watered intermittently to aid germination and establishment.

Success of the wildflower meadow

The results within the Memorial Park were outstanding and a full complement of red annuals could be seen from June to August. The seed burden on the roundabout did indeed prove to be too great; wildflower areas were achieved, but the results were noticeably different to those in the park.

Though wildflower earth does have some associated risks, a full meadow from seed to flower can be achieved in one growing season. To make sure they are affordable for district councils, costs need to be kept low as annual wildflower displays are only successful for a year at a time unlike perennials, which once established will return year after year. The annuals in this particular meadow were fantastic for impact and captured the public's imagination, helped by signage and publicity about the meadow in the local press. While poppies were essential in conveying the commemoration message, other red wildflowers were needed to ensure a full season of flowering, since poppies are notoriously very short-lived. The meadow was situated within an urban park where daily footfall is very high. The success of the meadow is largely due to the respect that the public had for this beautiful display; at no point throughout the summer were the wildflowers trodden on.

In this case, wildflower earth required simple preparation, with one application of glyphosate to the area with no requirement for rotovation.

After the layer of earth has been spread evenly, gentle watering is required.

Opposite: The resultant poppy meadow in the park was spectacular.

Above: Where sow thistle had crept into the area in the first year, the second year's display was dominated by the weed.

Right: The roundabout display, while effective, never quite made the impact of the park owing to inadequate treatment prior to the earth installation.

CASE STUDY 23

Regenerating a city site

The greening of brownfield sites

LOCATION Brownfield sites in Sheffield.
PURPOSE To inspire a community to enjoy their outside space and enhance their quality of life with temporary landscapes before redevelopment.
INSTALLATION METHOD Annual seeding.
SPECIFIC CHALLENGES Working within highly populated areas with the aim of encouraging an interest in green space from local residents.
AREA Plots of 500 sq m (598 sq yd).

In recent years, Sheffield City Council has been responsible for a huge area of land that is awaiting redevelopment. Such brownfield sites are often magnets for fly-tipping and other antisocial behaviour and the quality of life for residents was low, as was developer confidence in building there. A temporary solution was needed to improve the area with the aim of making it more attractive for private investment in housing development. Council confidence in any greening project was lacking and a solution that was both cheap and immediate was required. An initial three-year strategy of using seed-sown meadows on a huge scale started in 2004 and is still continuing at the time of writing, 11 years later. In order to encourage the public to understand and support the work, local schools and community groups were invited to become involved in the easy process of sowing annual seed on the relatively small start-up areas.

JAMES SAYS . . .

Whatever the project, it is natural for the people involved to want to see results that justify their interest and excitement. This project is a classic example of the way to engage and enthuse people with the benefits of urban greening. Involving the community from the start wins hearts and minds and giving a sense of ownership ensures interest and a far greater likelihood of long-term success. It is acceptable that plants take time to flower, but it mustn't take too long and the results must be good, otherwise enthusiasm quickly wanes and an opportunity is lost. This is always a danger with any natural planting and choosing reliable establishment techniques is the most important decision in any development. In this case the annuals are very reliable and as a short-term option they fit the bill perfectly.

Changing the space from run-down and ignored to appreciated and enjoyed also helped to put the developers at ease for the work to go ahead. The local community has bought into this project and it opens the door for longer-term solutions in the future.

Installation

Site preparation in the early years was the greatest challenge as the ground was a mix of demolition rubble, fly-tipped debris, underground services and abandoned back gardens. The main cultivation activities were focused on clearing all protruding materials within the top 150 mm (6 in). Once the areas were cleared, plots were allocated to various groups who were able to broadcast annual seed. School classes would share out the seed and walk in lines treading in the seed as it was sown in spring. Green Estates managed the entire project, planning the areas sown, the seed mixes used and the establishment and maintenance regimes. Over the years sowings have taken place from early March right through to mid-June in all kinds of weather and success levels have been consistently high.

Success of the wildflower meadow

The vibrant colour of annuals will always evoke a strong reaction but the surprise was the high degree of positivity that they conjured in the local community and outsiders too. While there were a few areas that were abused and plenty of flowers were picked to take home, for the most part the meadows looked great. No fencing was required as it was found that few people actually want to play in mud and so the seed established well. It was important to consider desire lines and over the years careful consideration has been given to planning pathways to encourage people into the meadow areas. Mown edges defined the meadow areas and once the flowers were established, the height of the vegetation generally deterred people from wading through it.

By November each year, the annuals start to look scruffy and so they are completely cut down and left dormant over the winter period to start the regime again in March. From the third year onwards, a system of checking annual weeds was started in order to reduce the build-up of undesirable species. In some cases this involved a one-off pull of some large weeds such as fat hen while in others a total cut at early emergence was made, with the blades set high to check the faster weed growth and allow the slower slender annuals to thrive.

This temporary solution to change struggling neighbourhoods is now a strategy that has been used extensively. The annual plantings both transform the appearance of previously neglected areas and bring about a marked reduction in antisocial behaviour.

There was little to benefit anyone or anything before the start of this landscaping project.

Left: The site was cleared by an army of enthusiastic sowers.

Below: They soon saw the advantages of their work as butterflies were found in the meadow.

Right: Luckily establishment is sufficient that some losses go unnoticed.

Woodland meadow

Creating a wildflower landscape in reclaimed woodland

LOCATION The garden of a children's hospice in a reclaimed woodland area, West Sussex.

PURPOSE To make a stimulating space for seriously ill people.

INSTALLATION METHOD Wildflower turf.

SPECIFIC CHALLENGES Designing features to allow those in wheelchairs an immersive experience.

AREA 125 sq m (150 sq yd)

Chestnut Tree House is a children's hospice caring for more than 300 children and young adults with progressive life-shortening conditions. The staff strive to make every day count and the new outdoor area needed to reflect that ethos. The project became the forty-third garden that was part funded by the Greenfingers charity and helped by donations to the Chestnut Tree Hospice.

Family and staff were asked to contribute ideas for fundraising and for the design of the garden. Ann-Marie Powell, a prolific garden designer, was brought on board to design a garden covering 2.5 sq km (1 sq mile) that included a sensory woodland walk with picnic areas, an amphitheatre, a wildlife pond and bug hotels. Many of the residents are wheelchair-bound and the designs had to allow them access and give them the feeling of being immersed in nature. The wildflower area was designed as an amphitheatre so that those children who were unable to sit or lie in the meadow would still be able to see flowers and grasses above their eyeline to help them too feel close to the natural world.

JAMES SAYS . . .

This was a sensitive project and it was vitally important that the meadow was a success from the start. The landscaper involved had been on a specific wildflower installation training programme so we knew the project was in safe hands. The use of wildflowers on banks to provide an immersive experience was inspired design; we know that wildflowers not only can provide a sense of well-being but the sounds, feel and smell of the meadow all help to awaken the senses. While most meadows are now part of a managed landscape, it never ceases to amaze me how satisfying it is to be within a seemingly wild environment. It was lovely to hear how this environment has benefited the children at Chestnut Tree House.

Installation

Garden House Design, a local landscape contractor, took on this prestigious project. Access for the contractor and their equipment was very difficult due to the woodland area. The slopes of the amphitheatre needed stabilizing and using turf ensured there was no soil erosion despite heavy rain after installation. The speed of maturity of the meadow meant the area was in use two days after the contractors were finished.

Success of the wildflower meadow

Emma Hanford from Greenfingers charity says, 'With the wildflower turf, we have created a beautiful banked amphitheatre area where the hospice children and families can see flowers and the variety of insects they attract right up close. They can learn about and engage with nature through the seasons and enjoy spending time outdoors in the fresh air.'

Top: Eye-level wildflower growth helps immerse visitors in nature.

Above: Walkways ensure easy wheelchair access to all areas of this woodland site.

Overleaf: This beautiful garden is designed to provide multi-sensory stimulation to visitors.

Enhanced meadows

A meadow should be seen as an ongoing project that can be enhanced and developed over the years. Whether it is new or old, there are many ways to improve the species diversity and the overall visual impact of your space. Using an established meadow as a canvas on which to work for the benefit of species diversity can be rewarding both aesthetically and as a study in nature.

A perennial meadow provides you with plenty of opportunity to experiment. If you are not happy with the species diversity, plugging with established plants is a great way of introducing new species or even controlling grass dominance. Adding bulbs and pathways can be simple small projects to keep your meadow in good shape and interesting throughout the year.

Plug plants extend the flowering season and increase the flower content of a meadow which is good for pollinators and people.

From pastureland to wildflowers

Converting pastureland to a wildflower meadow

LOCATION Marshy grassland in rural southern England.
PURPOSE To create a meadow out of existing grasslands.
INSTALLATION METHOD Plug plants.
SPECIFIC CHALLENGES Controlling a fertile grassy field to aid wildflower growth.
AREA 629 sq m (752 sq yd).

Souren Ala, an experienced meadow-maker, was appointed by clients in north Hampshire to help convert an existing area of pastureland to wildflower meadow. The area had quite a range of characteristics, from wet boggy land to areas underlying mixed woodland which was mostly dry and shaded. The grass was well established and the soil was known to have high fertility. The area had been occasionally grazed and given an annual cut. The owners are keen conservationists and were opposed to using herbicides. As they wanted to take the area back to a traditional meadow on a limited budget, it was decided that naturalizing the grassland with the addition of plug plants was the way forward.

Souren chose a plug plant supplier who offered a range of plants for different conditions. In total Souren specified 3000 plants and while many of the species suited the individual areas and their conditions, he also added some species from a wish list to provide extra colour, such as scabious and knapweed, hoping they would thrive in these conditions. He worked to a grid system to get an even spread of plugs.

Installation

The grass was mown very short in October and plugs were planted at 40 cm (16 in) intervals along a tape. The plants were relatively small, in pots no larger than 25 cl (3 in), and tools similar to a bulb planter were used to dig out the holes ready to plant the plugs. It took two workers two full days to complete the planting. There was no need for irrigation in autumn. At the same time, Souren sowed areas of yellow rattle seed to help keep grass growth under control. The area was then fenced off to protect it from deer and left alone over winter.

After the site was checked in February it appeared that the seeded yellow rattle had not germinated very well and Souren decided to buy established yellow rattle attached to a host grass and plant them into the meadow as an additional grass controlling method.

Success of the wildflower meadow

Nine months later the grass was still very much the dominant plant within the meadow and the owners started a hand-pulling regime in June to thin out the bigger clumps. In places, the plugs had taken but there hadn't so far been much of a show of colour. The grass had grown faster than the plug plants and shrouded any wildflowers, making them less noticeable. However, the clients are very committed to their meadow and they have the time and enthusiasm to be very involved – they are in it for the long haul. They are still confident that over time they will achieve a biodiverse meadow but are very aware of the challenge it will provide and the time that they will need to commit to it.

JAMES SAYS . . .

It is clear that soil fertility is having a great effect on grass growth, limiting the success of the plug plants. A mild winter can have the same effect as the grasses will continue to grow through the winter and out-compete wildflowers. Seeding with yellow rattle is a lauded method to deplete grass due to the parasitic nature of yellow rattle, which lives off the grass, but we know that seed quality can be variable. We also know that yellow rattle seed requires an over-winter period of cold conditions to flower, and sowing in the autumn is definitely advised, as Souren did in this case.

To get on top of the grass growth I suggest that a strict regime of cutting and removing takes place at particular times of the year, the first being around June when grass growth is at its maximum. Cutting the sward to about 15 cm (6 in) and removing the cuttings will slow grass growth and give the wildflowers a chance to take hold. The second cut should be in the autumn, cutting and removing to 2.5 cm (1 in). The benefit of removing the grass when it is growing strongly is that you also remove the maximum amount of fertility from the soil. The plants will have taken up a lot of nutrients to achieve strong, lush growth and, by removing this nutrient-heavy top growth so it cannot break down into the soil, you successfully deplete fertility.

Naturalizing a meadow is a project for those with time on their hands but undoubtedly it will provide the owners with a huge amount of satisfaction as the site develops.

Top right: A large area of mown grass was cut right down in October to make the area ready for plugging.

Right: A wide selection of wildflower plugs were planted according to the different conditions in the area.

Top: The plug plants were evenly and accurately distributed throughout the area of the meadow.

Above: Yellow rattle was among the selected species, but this level of grass domination will take time to go down.

Right By the autumn, unchecked grass growth will be detrimental to the success of the plugs. A two-cut regime is in place, but consideration is being given to a more robust cutting plan of five or six cuts a season, at least for a few years to help the plugs get established.

Designer garden meadow

Turning a garden lawn into a wildflower meadow

LOCATION A suburban garden in Belgium

PURPOSE To create an enhanced meadow for a designer garden.

INSTALLATION METHOD Wildflower turf and spring- and summer-flowering bulbs.

SPECIFIC CHALLENGES Choosing the right bulbs to enhance the meadow

AREA 320 sq m (383 sq yd)

JAMES SAYS . . .

The garden owner's great ideas on how to design an area of garden to show off the wildflowers to their best and his ideas for including bulbs has been an inspiration for other sites. It has been exciting to see areas of wildflowers successfully installed both here and on other sites in Belgium and the Netherlands.

This showpiece garden in Shoten, Belgium earns its keep as a display piece for the owner who is a landscape and garden designer. He uses it throughout the year to demonstrate ideas to his clients. Having recently looked into naturalizing his planting schemes he decided to develop an area of the garden lawn into a wildflower meadow to showcase his ideas.

Installation

Wildflower turf was installed and spring and summer bulbs were designed into the project to add colour and interest. Some bulbs were installed before the turf was laid out and other bigger bulbs such as summer flowering alliums were dug in after the turf had established.

Success of the wildflower meadow

The area established quickly and is regularly used to demonstrate the benefits and possibilities available with this style of naturalized planting. As with most landscape professionals, the owner requires a system

that will work in a short time period without the need for too much follow-up work. Using the turf achieved this, as did enhancing it with bulbs. The meadow has been a particular success and has inspired a number of meadow instalments in the region.

Far left: The wildflower meadow soon after installation in the Belgian garden.

Above: The first summer's growth took over from the flowering spring bulbs.

Left: The meadow in full flower proved a delight for the owner.

Top: Summer bulbs such as liatris have added to the diversity and interest of the garden.

Right: Mown paths make access easy to allow full appreciation of the diversity of the planting.

Far right: Species-rich planting will always complement a pond or river and result in a wildlife-friendly habitat.

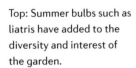

Multi-habitat meadow

Enhanced planting using bulbs and wildlife-friendly native species from seed and turf

LOCATION A large domestic garden with a riverside location.

PURPOSE To create a native meadow with year-round appeal for humans and wildlife.

INSTALLATION METHOD Wildflower turf, a seeded growing mix, spring bulbs and plugs.

AREA 600 sq m (718 sq yd).

The owner was keen to adopt a holistic approach to creating a meadow and began the project by consulting a local wildflower expert. He recommended using plug plants that had been grown from locally sourced seed and then leaving the whole area to grow wild. However, yellow rattle seemed to have little impact on the rampant grass growth and another approach was required. Keen to see more of a meadow in a shorter timescale, the owner researched further methods of establishment and decided to use a mix of wildflower turf and wildflower-seeded earth to create a pattern of wildflowers, continuing with locally sourced plants where possible. It was hoped to then encourage the spread of those species into adjacent areas by using a number of enhancement techniques.

The owner and her advisor assessed the species in the wildflower turf and it was agreed that a combination of locally sourced wildflower seed and plugs grown from some of that seed would supplement the newly established turf. In addition, a pre-seeded growing medium would be used in certain sections and

JAMES SAYS . . .

The multi-pronged approach to establishing different areas of wildflowers has been interesting to follow in this project, which is still developing. Prior to the current owner's arrival the extensive garden was very short of species diversity, with a large area of mown lawn surrounded by grass paddocks and agriculture. A small water meadow provided some good biodiversity and the new wildflower areas now link this to the woodland and the river, resulting in a garden of many types of habitat, colour and diversity.

The owner's continuing interest in the natural environment and enthusiasm for the meadow will help to expand its size and diversity. Already the garden has become a haven for wildlife and gets the very best out of the various habitats.

the whole area would be underplanted with spring-flowering bulbs.

Installation

A two-spray programme of glyphosate was used to clean up grasses and weeds prior to rotovating the site and raking it even. After scattering a mix of bulbs on the prepared soil, the family laid the turf with the help of a gardener. The bulbs were kept to early-flowering varieties with subtle colours, although the wetter areas were treated slightly differently, using fritillary at a generous rate. Once laid, the turf was plugged with some home-grown devil's-bit scabious (*Succisa pratensis*) plants.

Success of the wildflower meadow

The bulbs have been very successful and have required no maintenance. The wildflowers took over from the bulbs to give a long season of colourful flowering with a mow and remove in the autumn as a one-cut maintenance programme.

The turf areas have worked well. The wildflower-seeded earth has also given great results, although it looked slightly different in the first year due to a lower rate of grass in the seed mix resulting in a more open sward. In this section of the garden, the devil's-bit scabious plugs have been slow to establish and make an appearance but there is still evidence of the plugged plants and time will tell as to their success.

The owner is passionate about the meadow areas in the garden and has a great knowledge of wildflowers, while taking additional advice from designers and wildflower experts on how to encourage them. In the water-meadow area where a naturalizing approach has been taken the introduction of additional plugs has worked to a limited degree, but yellow rattle seed has established well and is now having a positive effect on reducing the grass growth.

Soil preparation is well underway, with a second dose of glyphosate ready to apply.

Above: In the first spring after the start of the project, the combination of wildflower turf, fritillaries and wet soil produce exceptional results.

Left: The regimented approach to initial establishment is quickly softened as seed heads are encouraged to spread into adjacent areas as a method of expanding the size of the meadow.

Above: In the second year, the cutting regime and enhancement techniques have help to expand the margins of the meadow through naturalizing.

Left: The consistently damp soil favours moisture-loving species such as this ragged robin. As these species produce seed, it is collected and encouraged in other less diverse areas in the garden as a simple but effective enhancement technique.

Modern meadow

Immersing a new house in a new meadow

LOCATION Southern England.
PURPOSE To nurture a wildlife habitat that blends the house into the landscape.
INSTALLATION METHOD Wildflower turf.
SPECIFIC CHALLENGES To meet the expectations of the owners who set a challenging design brief that grew out of their love of wildflowers, interest in the history of meadows and desire to help nature.
AREA 950 sq m (1136 sq yd).

Michael and Phil took over an existing farm in Berkshire to create their new home and premises for their micro-brewery, Two Cocks Brewery. The existing farm had been over-grazed and left generally untouched for more than 15 years, with no addition of fertilizer. This meant the site should be ideal for wildflowers. The modern design of the new house and the inclusion of walls built entirely from flint led to the decision to develop a wildflower meadow to soften lines and help the house merge into the landscape. Michael and Phil felt a mown lawn would have looked wrong as well as being a great deal of work. They also had grazing for their sheep to consider.

The building work had led to the creation of some steep banks and turf seemed to be the ideal solution in order to immediately stabilize the areas surrounding the house as well as to provide useful weed control on soil that would provide the opportunity for weed seeds to germinate if left alone. The progress of the garden would be conducted under the scrutiny of the TV series Grand Designs.

JAMES SAYS . . .

This is a great case study for many reasons. It is lovely to find people who are so dedicated to their meadow. Our first encounter with Michael and Phil brought much excitement as this project was part of the television series Grand Designs, but the programme came and went and the follow-up with the pair has shown that this was not about cosmetics for the cameras but a genuine love for nature. It is always fabulous to get feedback that observes the value a wildflower meadow can bring not only to its owners but also its tenants – the owls and other animals that have been observed by Michael and Phil as a result of providing suitable habitat.

And I admire anyone who is prepared to step back in time and work with a scythe! However, whether scythes, strimmers or self-propelled machines are used, the important thing is to cut and remove in the autumn. A very good point is made about developing a programme of sequential cuts for the benefit of the wildlife. This also contributes to enhancing the meadow, as the various cutting times will influence the flowering duration. Such experimentation will lead to long-term improvements in the ornamental value of the meadow. I really look forward to hearing how this project progresses over the years.

Installation

The site was thoroughly watered before and after the turf was laid in autumn, with the idea that it would have a year to get underway prior to allowing sheep to graze on the land the following autumn. It is a substantial area of garden but the wildflowers fitted with the ethos of Michael and Phil's business and the meadow quickly became much more than a garden. They admit it is a way of life, to the extent that they now describe it as an obsession!

Success of the wildflower meadow

Michael and Phil took an early decision to maintain the meadow in a traditional manner and enrolled on a scything course. They felt that scything rather than strimming would be much kinder to the wildlife and would encourage a more diverse display as well as being much quieter and providing the mind and body with a wonderful workout! In total they dedicate about 12 days to scything in four stages, raking up the arisings for seed collection for sowing in an adjacent area in order to create a new meadow. After each area has been scythed, sheep are allowed onto it from July to October to keep the growth in check. Different patterns of growth are visible according to the date of scything. Growth is a lot less dense in the more shaded areas behind the house, which is particularly noticeable when scything as opposed to strimming. Different species tend to dominate in different areas, which Michael and Phil think may be to do with the varying scything times. The growth in the first year was completely different to that of the second year, due to extreme rainfall in the first year; the second year's growth was much slower and less rampant.

While Michael and Phil commit a great deal of time to their meadow they feel it is an acceptable amount of work that fits with their way of life; they are looking forward to seeing how it evolves over time. In the second year they added mown pathways in order to access different areas of the garden and enable the dogs to roam more easily as they felt walking freely through it would create damage to the plants over time. They are also in the process of adding further diversity to the species and have plugged fritillary and wild orchids into certain areas. This year they have undertaken a special flower pressing project that will enable them to record their meadow development week by week. They scan their meadow for newly flowering plants and press the flowers in date order.

Clearly Michael and Phil are thoroughly committed to their meadow and when asked what the overriding feature of the meadow was they replied, 'its ability to make you very happy'. They see themselves as guardians of their space and it is important to them to 'tread carefully'. An extra pleasure is that the meadow has become a hunting ground for tawny owls, little owls and barn owls, which are regularly seen ghosting over the meadow along with increased populations of bats.

Left: A programme of sequential scything has enhanced the look of the meadow, as well as its value to wildlife.

Below left: The TV programme came and went but the natural setting continued to develop, as did Michael and Phil's love for their home's peaceful and tranquil atmosphere.

Right: The close proximity of the wildflowers to the house makes for easy and undisturbed wildlife viewing.

Below: The overall impression of this contemporary new build is one of long-established peace and tranquillity

Iconic meadows

I have been lucky enough to be involved in some very interesting wildflower projects since starting the soil-less wildflower system. Some have been one-off events that have helped to raise awareness and interest in wildflowers and others are projects that I have witnessed from the start, watching them establish and grow over a number of years. This has not only helped me to develop a way of establishing meadows that can be used with confidence, it has also given me the delight of revisiting some beautiful wildflower spaces.

For various reasons the case studies in this section stand out to me as flagship projects. Some have changed the hearts and minds of the public worldwide and inspired many to create their own meadows. One is a hidden gem showing long-term commitment to a meadow and providing vast knowledge in the maintenance of a perennial wildflower landscape. And finally, there is a personal story of the first meadow I created, pioneering a wildflower system that has gone on to be used throughout Europe. They have all played a part in developing my knowledge and enthusiasm for creating wildflower meadows.

Public interest in iconic meadows like this one at the London Olympics in 2012, has lead to renewed interest in the meadow environment.

A meadow restored

Restoring a historic garden to its former glory

LOCATION Rural landscape, southern England.

PURPOSE To restore a former meadow landscape.

INSTALLATION METHOD A mix of wildflower turf and seeding over a 10-year period.

SPECIFIC CHALLENGES Creating and maintaining a meadow landscape on a large scale.

AREA 10.4 ha (25 acres)

When the current owner took over the property the gardens were a little neglected, though beautifully designed and sympathetic to the ideals of William Robinson and Miss Jekyll. Looking back through historical pictures, the owner decided that she would like to restore the meadow areas to their former glory and went about researching reinstatement methods. Within the garden there are two main meadow areas, one visible from the house and the other a wider expanse of land that is hidden among trees. It was decided that the visible area needed to be established as quickly as possible, so wildflower turf was chosen. The larger hidden meadow was to be a longer term project that would be established with locally sourced seed. The estate manager had previously tried wildflower plugs to create a meadow and knew that on this scale it would be impossible.

Installation

The turf installation was relatively straightforward. With lawn having preceded it, a simple spray-off with glyphosate and rotovation was all that was required. The larger seeded area took a great deal more work to spray off and plough the area, then rotovate and seed it. This was followed by extensive maintenance, with regular cutting and removing over a number of years.

Success of the wildflower meadow

After four years of intensive management, the seeded meadow is fully established and both areas are cut by a hay contractor in early July, using a specific hay mower to take the meadow back to 10 cm (4 in). There is certainly a higher grass content in the seeded meadow and patching areas with yellow rattle is making an improvement where there is grass domination. Both meadows looked heavy with ox-eye daisies during the early years but over time there has been a noticeable decrease in the volume with more species diversity being apparent through June.

A further maintenance cut in late February is also used to keep the grass growth in control. This takes the sward back to a very low level and means that both grass and wildflowers start the growing season at the same level. It also has the added advantage of exposing patches of earth, often made by moles, that can then be treated early by seeding.

The success of the meadow is without question due to the commitment and expertise the estate manager has given to the area over the years. The turf was a reliable solution and from year one provided an established meadow that the owner could look out on from the house, providing much pleasure. In the years since the turf was laid, the estate manager reports further flower species being seen. The seeded meadow took 3–4 years of mowing, removal of cuttings, weeding and caring, along with a huge amount of knowledge

This is a wonderful case study that compares the two different techniques of establishment in this sympathetic restoration of a historic landscape, taking it back to how it would have looked 100 years ago. Having supplied the wildflower turf and seed in 2009, we have been very fortunate to monitor the progress of this meadow and have the benefit of the estate manager's help and expert opinions. Seeing the two systems side by side has reiterated the value of both wildflower turfing and wildflower seeding. To have success on this scale, knowledge, patience and commitment to an ongoing maintenance regime is required whichever system is used.

As a nation, we are lucky to have enthusiasts like the owner and estate manager. They are real guardians of the land, keeping large-scale meadows alive and setting a standard that others can achieve.

Above: In June, the wildflower turf is laid between existing grass paths.

Opposite top and below: Within four weeks of laying the turf the flowers have emerged, although over-wintering is needed for full species development.

of what to weed and what to preserve. There is now little difference between the two meadows and the ultimate success is the sheer magnitude of the expanse of wildflowers, truly a visual treat through spring and summer. It has been a magnet for birds of prey, including kites and barn owls, along with a thriving population of amphibians. There have also been sightings of a huge variety of solitary bees including the black ground bee and the leaf cutter bee.

Top: In the second year of turf establishment, well-managed paths provide a contrast between formal and wild.

Above: The seeded area developed well under a regime of regular cutting and removing and weeding for the first three years of its life.

Above right: In maturity the area is a well-tended biodiverse wildflower meadow.

Left: By year four, the seeded area was thriving and a beautiful and extensive meadow was in place.

Below: Grass domination in places is being treated with the colonization of yellow rattle.

Bottom: The results of both wildflower turf and seed are of an exceptionally high standard, using techniques that can be employed to create meadows anywhere and on any scale.

Olympic meadow

Creating a movable pictorial meadow as a one-off set dressing

LOCATION London 2012 Olympics, Opening Ceremony.
PURPOSE To depict England's 'Green and Pleasant Land'.
INSTALLATION METHOD A mix of different types of turf from annual flowering meadows.
SPECIFIC CHALLENGES A demanding remit of colour and variety. Appalling weather during turf growth, with a non-negotiable installation date.
AREA 10,000 sq m (11,960 sq yd).

This was a turfing project with a difference! We have supplied many film and stage productions with our turf over the years, but this was on an altogether different scale. This once-in-a-lifetime project left no room for error, with the ceremony being televised to billions around the globe. A number of different types of species-rich turf were developed in order to meet the demands of Danny Boyle and the creative team of the 2012 Opening Ceremony.

The famous grassy hill known as the 'Tor' was covered with our wildflower roof turf, which was designed to be drought-tolerant. Two months prior to the ceremony, this turf was attached to the prefabricated fibreglass Tor, with no underlying soil and only capillary matting for a root zone.

The annual flower turf was designed to be full of colour, a mass of bright flowers framing the set on which dancers, animals, athletes and dignitaries introduced our country and the 2012 Olympics to the world. This colourful annual turf was also used in 'The Smallholding' around the cottage.

JAMES SAYS...

Creating this iconic meadow was far from the norm when establishing a wildflower environment. Starting with the Opening Ceremony, the landscape of the 2012 Olympics has rekindled a passion and desire for wildflowers. Its sustainable and ecological theme can be seen as a turning point after years of decline and disregard for such an important habitat, and this legacy continues today.

A grassy perennial turf was grown to cover the running track. Here the athletes, complete with national flags, waited until the flag bearer moved on to plant the flag in the Tor. There was also a small area of long grass for the sheep paddock and despite concerns for the welfare of the sheep during the ceremony they could be seen happily grazing away, oblivious to the noise and packed crowds.

Installation

For a 'one night only' installation, the practicalities of laying the turf were rather different to normal landscaping requirements. For example, the steep slopes of the Tor had no soil and the capillary matting and turf were screwed to the fibreglass using thousands of steel self-drilling screws. This area was laid two months in advance of the ceremony and with the spring and summer of 2012 being cold and wet, there was no need to water until ten days before the games when the

Above: Annual wildflower turf loaded on stillages (trays) for delivery to the Olympic stadium.

Right: The turf was installed one week before the Opening Ceremony.

rain eventually eased up. When the sun did come out, the turf quickly dried out and required daily watering to keep it looking fresh, but the outcome was spectacular, with a mass of flowering plants and long grasses.

The perennial grasses and wildflowers for the athletes' standing areas were installed a week before the Games, as were the annual flowering turf that was laid on the slope around the stage where the main ceremony took place. This gave time for the plants to settle and 'stand up' so that they looked as if they had been there for years. The flowering turf was delivered on stillages (large, self-supporting trays) so that the plants weren't squashed, and were handled gently to keep them intact.

The main stage was where the challenges really started. The nature of the opening ceremony meant there were set transformations through the evening, so in advance of the games each phase required a number of rehearsals, all carefully planned to give everyone time to practise. We supplied a lot of turf that was used only for rehearsals where the volunteers were shown how and when to lift the turf away. The moving of turf and materials then transformed the stage into its next phase, from 'Green and Pleasant Land' to 'The Industrial Revolution'. During the dress rehearsal we were reprimanded for supplying turf that was too short for the sheep pen, only to find out later that the sheep had eaten it all!

Installing the turf was necessarily a matter of the last few minutes. We had been asked to supply all of the stage set turf in 2 sq m (2½ sq yd) slabs for quick installation and removal, a very speedy Industrial Revolution! The nature of the soil-less turf provided a clean and relatively light mat of plants – a significant help considering there has never been so much time pressure on a turf installation and revamp project.

Success of the wildflower meadow

The Opening Ceremony of the London 2012 Olympic Games was heralded as the best ever. The 'Tor' was the iconic backdrop to the entire show, which culminated in every competing nation placing their flag on a path leading to the top. Various celebrities said their piece, all framed by the wildflowers grown on our farm.

Left: The Tor before...

Below: ...and after installation.

Opposite right: The Tor during the ceremony.

Opposite below: Lifting the turf into position.

Left: The crowds arriving at the stadium are greeted by a green and pleasant land . . .

Below left to right . . . complete with rain clouds . . .

. . . and sheep . . .

. . . before the Industrial Revolution tears the rural idyll apart.

The Tor remained in place through the night.

Roadside wildflowers

Beautifying the roadsides of a northern town

LOCATION Rotherham roadside verges

PURPOSE To change opinion about the way in which roadside verges can be managed.

INSTALLATION METHOD Annual seeding.

SPECIFIC CHALLENGES Working on busy roads and converting miles of neatly mown amenity grass to annual flowers.

AREA 7000 sq m (8372 sq yd) along 8 miles of road.

In 2013, Rotherham Borough Council decided to change the way they managed their verges. The verges had been mown 8–10 times a year, leaving a grass verge of limited species diversity and no interest for the public; the aim now was to increase biodiversity and public enjoyment while at the same time saving money on maintenance contracts. The council took the bold move to transform 8 km (5 miles) of inner ring road into a River of Flowers – a very ambitious project because of the scale of planting and the fact that this was a radically different approach to the look and management of roadside verges.

Installation

Rotherham Borough Council commissioned Pictorial Meadows to install and maintain a meadow on the site, installation required road closures and night working for the course of one week. The existing vegetation had been sprayed off in early spring and again four weeks before ground preparation took place. Compact tractors were used to rotovate the verges and to get a good firm seedbed the verges were ring-rolled with a Cambridge roller. Sowing took place immediately after this with a mechanical seed sower. Soil movement and seed blowing was feared but in fact there was very little damage to the verges while the seeds germinated. There was no follow-up aftercare and no irrigation was needed.

The seed mix included both native and selected non-native annual wildflowers which provided an extended period of nectar, flowers and seeds that are food sources for many pollinating insects, birds and even some mammals. At the end of a long flowering season the vegetation was flailed and left in situ. The scheme was repeated in exactly the same way in years two and three, with some new areas being brought into the scheme and a few areas left to regenerate by self-seeding.

Success of the wildflower meadow

At the time this project was the largest local authority high-impact meadow highway scheme in the UK and it was a precursor to many others. It has enjoyed phenomenal public appreciation and built the confidence of the managers to extend the programme further afield, as well as winning the Green Apple Award for Environmental Best Practice. There have been significant financial savings by reducing the amount of grass cutting required and the scheme brought the added bonus of urban biodiversity.

Top right: There is not a lot to recommend this council verge, which is like thousands of others.

Centre right: The experts arrive to start the transformation.

Bottom: The verge has been seeded with a mix of native and non-native annual wildflowers.

JAMES SAYS . . .

This is a large-scale project and its success is generating interest in urban biodiversity and colour. Seeing the results, it is hard to understand why this approach isn't embraced by all councils and anyone else responsible for a roadside verge.

Colour and biodiversity win with a project like this, but there are wider financial benefits too. Green space in housing developments can be justified by the extra value that can be added to the individual house prices, simply because the area is a nice place to live.

Additional health benefits are apparent. Research shows the potential for speedier recovery from illness where patients are close to green space and there are research studies underway to look at the capability of wildflowers to lock up pollutants and improve air quality. By examining vegetation growing in close proximity to the source of emissions, the study expects to show how the density and shape of the leaves of some wildflower species lock in the fine pollution particles that are so damaging to people's health.

Above: The dramatic
transformation has
provided inspiration
for the way roadside
verges can be used
to benefit urban
environments.

Right: This visual
display makes the area
a more desirable place
to live.

Opposite right: Studies
show that vegetation
in close proximity to
the source of emissions
will lock up harmful
pollutants and improve
air quality significantly.

Chelsea Flower Show meadow

A ground-breaking, award-winning Chelsea Garden

LOCATION RHS Chelsea.

PURPOSE To depict the Chatsworth House garden as a Show Garden.

INSTALLATION METHOD Wildflower turf plugged with further species.

SPECIFIC CHALLENGES Creating a garden that looked as if it had always been there in the space of three weeks.

AREA 300 sq m (359 sq yd).

The return of Dan Pearson to RHS Chelsea in 2015 was eagerly awaited, this time with his interpretation of the Paxton gardens at the Chatsworth Estate in Derbyshire. Dan has long been the flag-bearer for garden design inspired by nature, so it was with great excitement that we accepted the challenge to grow a native wildflower turf for this project. After a number of visits from Crocus, the contractor who would be installing the garden, a bed of turf was chosen and set aside over the winter of 2014–15. Contingency plans were made, but everyone hoped that the spring weather would be kind enough to bring the wildflowers on to be ready for the show in mid-May.

Installation

With just six days to go before the show, the site was finally ready to receive the turf. As with the Olympic Opening Ceremony, the only way to transport the turf was on stillages (trays), which allowed the contractors to lay it directly onto the site without damaging it. The weather leading up to the show had been cold, resulting in a thinner sward than expected. This suited Crocus as it allowed for the addition of a number of flowering plugs to increase the colour of the garden. The turf was laid in a week of full sun and required constant watering to bed in, but within six days the turf looked perfect, with plenty of campion and ragged robin flowering at just the right moment. The wildflower turf formed the basis for large sections of the garden with plug plants such as the candelabra primula *Primula* 'Inverewe' and aconite buttercup (*Ranunculus aconitifolius*) looking at home in the mix.

Success of the wildflower meadow

Bringing a show garden of this magnitude together in such a short period of time is not for the faint-hearted and the attention to detail was breathtaking, with the Crocus team working tirelessly to get the garden to perfection. Dan Pearson's passion for naturalism and his skill as a designer inspired this meeting point of nature and horticulture to make a garden that looked wild, even though it was entirely man-made. He hoped that stepping into this garden would make people feel closer to nature and without a doubt it did.

It is the balance of macro and micro design that leads to outstanding gardens. Here the macro view with the huge boulders forming the hard landscaping balanced the micro detail that can be seen in the complex communities of wildflowers seen in the smallest 15 cm (6 in) square of ground space. This empathetic attention to detail resulted in a stand-out winner of the Best in Show award at RHS Chelsea 2015.

Top: The wildflower turf arrives at Chelsea on trays ready to install.

Right: Manoeuvring the turf mats into position.

Bottom: Great attention was paid to detail as turf was trimmed and plugs were added.

JAMES SAYS . . .

We have supplied wildflower turf to many show gardens at many different shows, both in the UK and abroad, and it is always a tricky proposition. Meeting the designer's expectations isn't always easy and trying to do it to suit the time of year of the show and weather conditions needs some thought and planning. Our normal advice to the contractor would be to take the turf at least a month in advance in order to grow it on, but this project was too big for that so we relied on regular assessment of the turf and nature doing its bit. In the end, the turf was quite sparse due to a cold early spring, but the pink and white campions came out with three days to spare and the open sward allowed room for the prepared plugs to add some extra colour.

It was a privilege to be involved in this project and watch the public reaction to something that was far from the normal manicured plots that tend to dominate the garden design world. This was a ground-breaking project, placing nature and biodiversity at the top of the list for garden trends in the coming years while reinforcing a wider interest and awareness for wildflowers in general.

Opposite: Chelsea 2015, Dan Pearson's garden is given the Best in Show award.

Right: The pink and white campion provided a delicate backdrop to much of the garden.

Bottom left: Macro and micro elements of the design work beautifully together.

Bottom right: On site, further delicate perennials such as these candelabra primula were plugged into the turf.

Lakeside meadow

Naturalizing a new lake by surrounding it with a wildflower landscape

LOCATION Irrigation lake, Ashe Warren Farm.
PURPOSE To test the viability and longevity of the newly developed wildflower turf in 2003.
INSTALLATION METHOD Native perennial wildflower turf.
SPECIFIC CHALLENGES Heavy growth of weeds which needed to be suppressed.
AREA 400 sq m (478 sq yd)

There are a number of questions that we are regularly asked about the wildflower turf and resulting meadows. Having the confidence to answer them has been in no small part due to having this site of native perennial wildflowers. Established in 2003, using the first wildflower turf I grew as a trial, it has stood the test of time and continues to go from strength to strength, fulfilling its purpose of reassuring us that wildflower turf has longevity when establishing meadows.

Installation

As a first effort, in comparison to pristine lawn turf, the wildflower turf looked very shabby – in fact too rough to know what to do with it, or where to trial it. We had just built the lake for irrigation purposes and there was some bare soil available around the margin. We knew it had a significant weed burden but we wanted to check the turf's weed-suppressing capability, so we went ahead and laid the turf in March 2003.

To everyone's amazement the turf took off and produced an array of colour and species, starting with ragged robin only eight weeks after it was laid. I managed to persuade our sons, Will and Olly, to pose

JAMES SAYS . . .

This may not be an iconic meadow for many, but it is for me as it has given me the confidence to promote wildflowers as a long-term solution. While we have done much research and development over time since then, this particular meadow was the starting point for a product that makes the creation of meadows easily achievable for many people. I have every reason to believe this meadow will go on and on, and at 12 years old, it looks better than ever.

Will and Olly are now well into their teenage years. I had hoped to get them to pose in the meadow as a way of representing the time that had elapsed and the age of the meadow, but they are teenage boys so I am going to try when they want a favour...!

with it and and the photo of them has been much used over the years in all sorts of PR material.

Success of the wildflower meadow

While the area has grown over the years, and includes samples of all the types of turf we grew for the 2012 Olympics, the original area is a healthy, biodiverse native wildflower meadow that has impressed many, from seed suppliers and garden designers to ecologists and botanists.

For me, it has proved that wildflowers are a long-term option. The maintenance has been one cut and remove a year and nothing else. We have pulled the odd weed, but rarely, and while some years the meadow has shown species domination at certain times of the year, this dominance is never long term and diversity and colour returns, in the same year and over subsequent years. As time has gone by, we have seen different species putting in an appearance; in 2012, nine years after installing the turf, I saw for the first time the cowslips that were sown in the original turf seed mix. This reminds us how some wildflower seeds will stay dormant for a long period of time, waiting for the ideal opportunity to germinate.

Top right: Waterproof lining for the newly excavated irrigation lake.

Above: The first flowering, with two young admirers who are now teenagers.

Far right: In 2003, newly laid turf was fully established within six weeks.

Right: Over the years the lake has been much admired and gives us great confidence over the longevity of our product.

Below: A few years later, the well-established wildflowers needed very little attention.

Top: In 2015, species diversity has not only been maintained but also improved with the emergence of new species year on year.

Right: The introduction of a beehive in 2008 has led to some very tasty honey.

Conclusion

Until recently, there has been a tendency to think of wildflower meadows as a lost historical landscape, on which to ruefully look back, lament and dismiss as out of reach to all but the largest landowners. It is time to think again as there are now exciting opportunities to bring wildflowers to a much broader audience and grow them in a wide range of situations.

Establishing wildflowers in urban and suburban areas, not only provides a pleasing aesthetic and improves the health and well-being of us humans but it also increases biodiversity and habitats for the benefit of wildlife.

As well as making a very positive contribution to nature, wildflowers mitigate pollution, improve urban cooling, lower ground maintenance costs and brighten people's lives. There is good reason to think of wildflowers as the ecological saviours of the years ahead. The tide is turning as we move away from the manicured landscapes of the twentieth century and aspire to a more natural state.

The tranquillity of a meadow promotes a sense of well-being and encourages people to spend more time outdoors.

Establishing wildflowers has been difficult, and they have a name for being tricky at best, impossible at worst! Simple and reliable methods are needed to ensure success and new design ideas are required to make them appealing and accessible. I grew up in the English countryside surrounded by nature and want to encourage wildflower habitat creation in a way that is realistic and achievable. It is one thing to hand out a pack of wildflower seeds but quite another to see those seeds develop into a species-rich area that contributes to biodiversity, wildlife and people's well-being. Achieving a wildflower utopia will only be possible if modern ideas are adopted. By de-mystifying the whole process, from establishment to maintenance, I want to encourage more people to try it.

I hope the case studies have provided you with the inspiration to 'give it a go'. Remember that creating a meadow does not need to be complicated or daunting and should certainly not be seen as the preserve of experts. There are wildflower mixes and products to suit every situation, whatever the size or purpose of the project. From improved biodiversity to vibrant colour, low-maintenance to award winning garden design, a wildflower meadow must deliver from the outset if it is to remain in place for the long-term.

The key to a successful meadow is perfecting the establishment phase; get that right and the rest follows. Think carefully about your site and which method of preparation and establishment will give your meadow the best chance of success. Like any other plant or crop, if it gets off to a bad start you will spend years trying to correct it. If you can avoid the early establishment problems you will have created a landscape to enjoy for many years to come, with minimal work required to keep it at its best.

So I hope this book will inspire you to put wildflowers to the forefront of your gardening and landscaping plans. Establishing a wildflower meadow is one of the biggest contributions you can make to the future well-being of your family, your friends and your planet.

Encouraging children to appreciate wildflowers and nature is important for the future of our environment.

Resources

WILDFLOWER SEED SUPPLIERS

Germinal www.germinal.com
Grass and wildflower seeds.

Jelitto www.jelitto.com. Perennial seeds.

John Chambers Wildflower Seeds
www.johnchamberswildflowers.co.uk
Native British wildflower seeds.

Pictorial Meadows
www.pictorialmeadows.co.uk
Specialist in meadow seed mixes.

Naturescape www.naturescape.co.uk
Bulbs, seeds and plants.

Rigby Taylor www.rigbytaylor.com
European near-native and non-native
flower seeds.

WILDFLOWER TURF SUPPLIERS

Wildflower turf www.wildflowerturf.co.uk
The pioneers of wildflower turf who started
the wildflower turf industry in the UK

Wiggly Wigglers
www.wigglywigglers.co.uk
Turf suitable for small domestic projects.

WILDFLOWER EARTH SUPPLIERS

Wildflower turf www.wildflowerturf.co.uk
Wildflower pre-seeded growing mix.

PLUGS AND BULBS

Hardys Cottage Plants
www.hardys-plants.co.uk
Perennial and naturalizing plants.

Really Wild Flowers
www.reallywildflowers.co.uk
Wildflower seeds and plug plants.

JUB Bulbs, Holland www.jubholland.nl
Spring- and summer-flowering bulbs.

HYDROSEEDING

Hydro Turf www.hydroturf.co.uk
A respected advocate of the hydro seeding
method.

ECOLOGISTS

Biodiversity by Design
biodiversitybydesign.co.uk

ECOSA www.ecosa.co.uk

WILDFLOWER EXPERTS
– NON-COMMERCIAL BODIES

Plantlife www.plantlife.org.uk
Flora Locale www.floralocale.org

Royal Horticultural Society
www.rhs.org.uk

Wildlife Gardening Forum www.wlgf.org

LANDSCAPE PROFESSIONALS

Society of Garden Designers
www.sgd.org.uk

**British Association of Landscape
Industries** www.bali.org.uk

**The Chartered Institute of Ecology
and Environmental Management**
www.cieem.net

The Landscape Institute
www.landscapeinstitute.org

CONSERVATION AND WILDLIFE

Bumblebee Conservation Trust
bumblebeeconservation.org

Butterfly Conservation
butterfly-conservation.org

Hawk Conservancy
www.hawk-conservancy.org

Scything Association
scytheassociation.org

Weald and Downland Open Air Museum
www.wealddown.co.uk

Bat Conservation Trust www.bats.org.uk

WHERE TO SEE WILDFLOWER
MEADOWS IN THE UK

Foster's Greens Meadows, Droitwich
www.worcswildlifetrust.co.uk/reserves/
fosters-green-meadows

RHS Harlow Carr, Harrogate, North Yorks
www.rhs.org.uk/gardens/harlow-carr

RHS Wisley, Surrey www.rhs.org.uk/
gardens/wisley

Carr House Meadows, South Yorkshire
www.wildsheffield.com/reserves/carr-
house-meadows

Manor Park, Sheffield

Highgrove Gardens, Gloucestershire
www.highgrovegardens.com

Queen Elizabeth Olympic Park, London
queenelizabetholympicpark.co.uk

Great Dixter, East Sussex
www.greatdixter.co.uk

**The Dan Pearson and William Morris
Meadow at Compton Verney**
www.comptonverney.org.uk

Munsary Peatlands, Caithness, Scotland
www.plantlife.org.uk/nature_reserves/
munsary_peatlands

Teifi Marshes, Ceredigion, Wales
www.teifiriverstrust.com

**Weald and Downland Open Air Museum,
Chichester West Sussex**
www.wealddown.co.uk

Cliffs of Mohar, County Clare, Ireland
www.cliffsofmoher.ie

Greenwich Peninsula, London
www.greenwichpeninsula.co.uk

WHERE TO SEE GREEN ROOFS IN THE UK

**Alder Hey in the Park Childrens Hospital,
Liverpool**
www.alderhey.nhs.uk/alder-hey-in-the-park

**Cardiff Castle Visitor Centre, Cardiff,
Wales**
www.cardiffcastle.com

Peppa Pig World, Hampshire
paultonspark.co.uk

Index

Page numbers in *italic* type refer to pictures or their captions.

The months referred to in the book are based on growing meadows in England, primarily south-east England. For meadow-makers in other parts of the world the months should be substituted with seasons as follows:

January	mid-winter
February	late winter
March	early spring
April	mid-spring
May	late spring
June	early summer
July	midsummer
August	late summer
September	early autumn
October	mid-autumn
November	late autumn
December	early winter

Acknowledgements

This book owes much to the helpful and positive feedback that I have heard and noted since starting our wildflower business. I have listened to numerous experiences, good and bad, from those who decided to give wildflowers a go. Collating these observations, writing them down and adding the pictures has made the book, and I am very grateful to all the gardeners and landscape professionals who have contributed.

I want to thank everyone at Wildflower Turf Ltd for working so hard to help develop the business that has made this book possible. Thank you to Trevor Bendall who, apart from being production manager, has shown patience beyond the call of duty when modelling for the step by step photographs.

Anna Mumford at Filbert Press saw the potential for a practical wildflower book and gave me the opportunity to write one; she has continually helped and reassured along the way – thank you Anna.

Without Emma Lappin this book would not have happened. Many thanks for your organisational skills and well-thought-out approach to the writing process and for all your support, encouragement and hard work to get the book completed.

About the author

James Hewetson-Brown was an arable farmer before he started experimenting with wildflower meadows, determined to find an approach that works for a wide range of sites and expectations. Now his successful techniques and products are used to establish beautiful, biodiverse meadows in private gardens and public spaces. His wildflower turf is in much demand by garden designers and has featured in Chelsea Flower Show gardens and on the celebrated set for the opening ceremony of London's Olympic Games.

Picture acknowledgements

We are grateful to the following for permission to use photographs and illustrations on the following pages:

Frank Adriensens 3, 100 top, 210-213; Souren Ala front cover main picture, 9, 31 left, 123-125, 205, 207-209; Richard Ayles, Slate Grey Design 11; Juliet Caird 13 bottom right, 159-161, 251; Guy Collier Photography front cover bottom inset pictures, back cover 1st and 3rd image, 4-5, 43, 48 top, 51, 53, 56, 57, 62, 63, 66, 67, 70, 71, 72, 73, 76, 78, 94, 95, 97, 101, 102, 104, 105, 107, 109, 121 bottom, 183 top, 217, 220, 221, 229, 250; Val Compton 192-193; Lisa Cox Garden Design 113; Helen Elks Smith Garden Design back cover 2nd image 129, 140-141; Garden House Design 134, 135, 203, 204; Graduate Gardeners 103; Christine Hatt 175, 177 top; Abbey Hawthorne 222, 231-235; The Hawk Conservancy 23, 25 bottom, 249; Norma Holland 179; HPW Architects 154, 164-165; Hydroturf 33; Ross Jackson 172, 181; JUB Holland 98; Emma Lappin 12, 13, 241-243; Kate McCrae, 144-147; Sean McGeachy 137-139; Organic Roofs 156, 157; Pictorial Meadows back cover bottom image, 4, 26, 32, 37, 38, 40, 127-128, 131-133, 199-201, 237-239, 245-248; Piers Partridge 81; Shades of Green 117; Shutterstock 16 top, 24, 25 top right, 85, 106; Soup Architects 176, 177 bottom; Karen Thorpe 55, 75, 115; Wildflower Turf 18, 19, 21, 22, 24, 25, 30, 31, 34, 35, 47, 48 bottom, 50, 52, 58, 59, 82, 83, 100, 103, 108, 110, 111, 113, 115, 119, 120, 121, 142, 149, 151, 152, 153, 163, 165, 167, 168, 169, 170, 171, 185, 186, 187, 188, 189, 195, 196, 197, 215, 216, 225, 226, 227, 228